EVERY PERSON'S GUIDE TO
KABBALAH AND JEWISH MYSTICISM

Every Person's Guide to Kabbalah and Jewish Mysticism

Ron Isaacs

KTAV PUBLISHING HOUSE

Every Person's Guide to Kabbalah and Jewish Mysticism

KTAV PUBLISHING HOUSE

527 Empire Blvd

Brooklyn, NY 11225

www.ktav.com

orders@ktav.com

Ph: (718) 972-5449 / Fax: (718) 972-6307

Set in Arno Pro by Raphaël Freeman MISTD, Renana Typesetting

ISBN 978-1-60280-457-9

Printed and bound in the United States of America

Acknowledgements

I would like to thank Moshe Heller for his continued confidence in my work. My work with Ktav Publishing goes back several decades and he and his team have continued to produce quality books. I continue to be proud to be one of its authors. I also want to thank my wife Leora for the incredible amount of time she spent copy editing, critiquing, and helping to shape this book. Her efforts have made for a more engaging book that will help readers better understand the world of Jewish mysticism.

For Leora, my
eishet chayil

Contents

Introduction

The Hebrew word *kabbalah* is the term applied to the entire realm of Jewish mystical activity and its teachings. The word *kabbalah* itself derives from the Hebrew word "tradition" or "receiving." Whereas Jewish law and its codes focus on human behavior and rabbinic understanding of what God desires from human beings, *kabbalah* concentrates on the essence of the Supreme Being, the origin of the universe, the creation of human beings, the destiny of people and the universe, and the profound significance of the sacred Torah. Unlike the Jewish rationalists like Maimonides and Saadia Gaon, whose understandings of God were influenced by Greek philosophy and science, the Kabbalists rebelled against any attempt to reduce religion to intellectual or philosophical beliefs. They were more concerned with *feeling* God's nearness through experience rather than with analyzing God's relationship to man. According to tradition, the mystical philosophy of the *kabbalah* is hidden and unintelligible to those who have not been properly prepared and instructed in the so-called secret wisdom (*chochmah neestera*) often referred to by the abbreviation *chen* (grace). The phrase *yoday chen* alludes to those who are familiar with kabbalistic literature, its symbols and philosophy.

The Biblical roots of Jewish mysticism are clearly evident from the descriptions of the divine chariot in the first chapter of the *Book of Ezekiel*. In the book's opening chapter, Ezekiel receives his call to prophecy in the form of a vision while in a trance. The description of the Divine Glory is replete with splendors of flashing light, so brilliant that while the details are minutely revealed they are so dazzling that they cannot be clearly seen. In fact, the earliest Jewish mystics were known as *Merkavah* mystics – explorers of God's chariot (*merkavah*). They sought to understand and interpret the mystery of Ezekiel's vision of God. Ezekiel claimed to have seen the likeness of God upon His throne in heaven, and these early Jewish mystics wanted to know exactly what he saw.

Glimpses of *kabbalah* mysticism can also be found in Talmudic and Midrashic literature. First handed down orally to a chosen few and then committed to writing, the mystical interpretation of the Torah is principally embodied in the *Zohar* (brightness). This volume was revealed to the Jewish world in the thirteenth century by Moses De Leon, who claimed that the book contained the mystical writings of the second-century rabbi Simeon bar Yochai. The purpose of the *Zohar* was not to make the Bible easier to understand, but rather to find the secrets of the universe within the Bible., Interest in *kabbalah* became widespread beginning in the thirteenth century and reached a climax in Spain in the following two centuries. Then, after a lapse of a century, it re-emerged with heightened pitch in Safed, Israel.

Kabbalists have always been reticent about publicly teaching their mystical doctrines. Believing that their ideas were too daring for the average person to grasp, kabbalists were convinced that only the chosen in each generation were worthy of receiving the wisdom of Jewish mysticism. *Every Person's Guide to Kabbalah and Jewish Mysticism* is an introductory guide to understanding Jewish mysticism and the mystical experience. Its goal is to introduce readers to the basic mystical concepts, teachings and personalities that helped to shape the kabbalistic movement, in a user-friendly way. I hope that this book will help readers demystify Judaism's rich and complex mystical dimension and inspire them to pursue their spiritual journeys with even greater fervor as they continue to discover new secrets about God and the universe.

RONALD H. ISAACS

Roots of Jewish Mysticism: Ezekiel's Vision and Other Early Jewish Mystics

EZEKIEL'S VISION

Early Jewish mysticism had its roots in the graphic account of the prophet Ezekiel's vision of God. The vision appears in the opening chapter of the book of Ezekiel, at the commencement of his prophetic ministry. The vision is of a strange and mysterious apparition known as the *Merkavah*, the Divine Throne-Chariot. The attempt to understand and interpret the vision gave rise to an esoteric thought system known in rabbinic literature as *Ma'aseh Merkavah* (stories of the Divine Chariot), which became the root and core around which Jewish mysticism developed. This realm of study was reserved for people of the highest intellectual and moral development, based on realistic fears people with lesser ability could succumb to mental and emotional imbalance. The *Mishneh* (*Chagigah 2:1*) forbids the exposition of the Divine Throne by anyone except wise people with independent insight.

The *Merkavah* is distinguished by its mobility. Unlike Isaiah's vision of the Divine Throne (Isaiah 6) or any other prophetic visions which did not include any wheels, the Merkavah was a wheeled structure, drawn by four-faced living creatures.

Following is an excerpt from Ezekiel's remarkable vision:

....the heavens were opened, and I saw visions of God...And I looked and behold, a stormy wind came out of the north, a great cloud, with a fire flashing up, so that a brightness was round about it. And out of the midst as the color of electrum, out of the midst of the fire. And out of the midst thereof came the likeness of four living creatures. And this was their appearance: they had the likeness of a man. And every one of them had four faces, and every one of them had four wings. And their feet were straight feet; and the soul of their feet was like the sole of a calf's foot; and they sparkled like the color of burnished brass. And they had the hands of a man under their wings on their four sides; and as for the faces and wings of the four, their wings were joined one to another, and they did not turn when they went. As for the likeness of the living creatures, their appearance was like coals of fire, burning like the appearance of torches. It flashed up and down among the living creatures, and there was brightness to the fire, and out of the fire went forth lightning. And the living creatures ran and returned as the appearance of a flash of lightning. Now as I beheld the living creatures, behold one wheel at the bottom hard by the living creatures, at the four faces thereof. The appearance of the wheels and their work was like the color of beryl. When they went, they went toward their four sides. They did not turn when they went. Over the heads of the living creatures there was the likeness of a firmament, like the color of the terrible ice, stretched over their heads above. And under the firmament were their wings conformable the one to the other. And when they went, I heard the noise of their wings like the noise of great waters, like the voice of the Almighty, a noise of tumult like the noise of a host. When they stood, they let down their wings. And above the firmament that was over their heads was the likeness of a throne, as the appearance of a sapphire stone, and upon the likeness of the throne was a likeness as the appearance of a man upon it above (*Ezekiel*, Chapter 1).

Ezekiel may well have been one of the first prophets to have recorded an account of a direct mystical experience with God, but it is difficult to fully comprehend his vision which is the heavenly throne of God and the likeness of the glory of God. That said, later Jewish mystics considered Ezekiel to be the prototypic Jewish mystic.

It is important to understand Ezekiel's vision of God as expressed in the opening chapter of his book as his *idea of the image of God*. He only perceived a likeness of God. While it is believed that he came as close to God as any person ever did, God's Being ultimately remained mysterious. It was this mystery that early Jewish mystics tried to understand. A critical difference between Ezekiel and his successors is that while his was a spontaneous occurrence, they tried to imitate his experience through rigorous and demanding training. The earliest recorded attempts at consciously pursuing mystical, ecstatic states appear in the second century of the common era.

THE JOURNEY OF THE FOUR RABBIS

The first Jewish mystics lived in Palestine in the first and second centuries of the Common Era. Many of them belonged to a group who studied with Rabbi Yochanan ben Zakkai, the scholar who gained permission from the Romans to set up an academy of Jewish learning in Yavneh. This academy became the spiritual center of Judaism after the Jerusalem Temple was destroyed in 586 BCE.

Rabbi Yochanan and his disciples were profoundly influenced by Ezekiel's fantastic vision of the Divine Throne, and fervently desired to know and experience what heaven was like. They turned to a new field of thinking called Gnosticism, from the Greek word *gnosis,* meaning knowledge. The goal of Gnosticism was to impart knowledge about heaven and to offer instruction regarding the true essence of God and how to reach heaven. The Jewish *merkavah* mystics conceived the journey to heaven in terms of Ezekiel's vision of God's throne. Because the idea of the journey to heaven originated in Gnosticism, the approach of these early mystics is also known as Jewish Gnosticism.

One of the early masters of Jewish mysticism was Rabbi Akiba ben Joseph, a leading second century scholar, who practiced a visionary form of mystical experience. He prepared himself for his ascent to the heavens through asceticism and various purification rituals. He envisioned heaven as consisting of seven firmaments (heavens). He believed that there were seven palaces in the seventh heaven, and if one could reach the seventh heavenly palace in the seventh heaven one would see God's chariot and throne. He visualized himself ascending through seven heavens and through the seven palaces in the highest heaven (the *Aravot*), to gain access to God's heavenly throne. Frequently Rabbi Akiba and his three colleagues Elisha ben Avuyah, Simeon ben Zoma and Simeon ben Azzai would fast a few days, lay their heads between their knees and whisper hymns and songs, to put themselves in a trance in an effort to reach the *Aravot*.

Simeon ben Azzai was so devoted to Torah study that he never married, while Simeon ben Azzai was a master of Midrash (the art of explaining biblical verses). Elisha ben Avuyah was not as devoted to Torah study. Rather, his real interest lay in Greek philosophy and in Gnosticism. This raised doubts about the principles of Judaism and brought ben Avuyah to the verge of completely losing his faith and becoming a heretic.

Here is a description of the famous journey that the four rabbis took, as described in the Talmudic tractate of *Chagigah 14b*:

> Our rabbis taught: Four men entered the Garden (*i.e.*, Heaven), namely Ben Azzai and Ben Zoma, Acher (*i.e.*, Elisha ben Avuyah) and Rabbi Akiba. Rabbi Akiba said to them: When you arrive at the stones of pure marble, do not say 'water, water.' For it is said: One that speaks falsehood shall not be established before my eyes. (Psalm 101:7). Ben Azzai cast a look and died. Of him the Bible says: Precious in the sight of God is the death of his saints. (*Psalm 116:15*). Ben Zoma looked and became demented. Of him the Bible says: Have you found honey? Eat as much as is sufficient for you, lest you be filled therewith, and vomit it. (*Proverbs 25:16*). Acher mutilated the shoots. Rabbi Akiba departed unhurt.

Apparently, the mystical visionary experience was so strong that it overwhelmed all of Rabbi Akiba's three colleagues. Ben Azzai died in an ecstatic trance, and Ben Zoma lost his mental equilibrium.

Elisha ben Avuyah is defected from Judaism to the Roman camp. Subsequently his name was changed to *"Acher"* meaning "alien." He persecuted Jewish youth and helped the Romans close Jewish schools. In the Talmudic text, this was euphemistically referred to as the "cutting down of the shoots." Only Rabbi Akiba was apparently prepared for this mystical heavenly journey, able to survive it and to return to earth in peace.

Rabbinic views about whether the rabbis' journey was real or only imaginary differ. Rashi, the great medieval French commentator, asserted that the journey was real, while Rabbi Chananel thought it was simply a figment of their imaginations. Whatever the case, this Talmudic passage came to serve as a warning to all future seekers not to pursue a mystical journey without the knowledge and stability to withstand it.

SEFER YETZIRAH

Known as the Book of Creation, *Sefer Yetzirah* is the earliest existing Hebrew text of systematic, speculative thought. The book has fewer than 2,000 words and appears in two versions: the shorter text that appears in most editions, and a longer version which is often printed as an appendix. Both versions were already in existence in the tenth century CE. The central subject of *Sefer Yetzirah* is a discourse on cosmology and cosmogony. The beginning of the book states that God created the world by means of 32 secret paths of wisdom. These 32 paths and the 22 letters of the Hebrew alphabet are represented as the foundations of all creation. Chapter 1 deals with the *sefirot* (translation) and the other five chapters with the function of the letters. The first four *sefirot* represent the four elements of the entire world: the spirit of God; ether (the spirit which is the world's atmosphere); water and fire. The following six *sefirot* represent the six dimensions of space.

There is no further mention of these *sefirot* in the rest of the book, which is devoted to a description of the roles of the Hebrew letters in creation. According to *Sefer Yetzirah,* the entire work of creation was enacted through the combinations of the Hebrew letters that were inscribed on the sphere of heaven and engraved into the spirit of God. The existence of every single creation depends on the combination of letters that lie hidden within it. This idea is very similar to the view advanced in the Talmudic tractate of *Berachot* 55a in the name of Rav, that there are "letters through which heaven and earth were created," and that the architect Bezalel built the tabernacle (which some asserted was a microcosmic symbol of the whole work of creation) through his knowledge of the combinations of these letters.

SEFER HABAHIR: THE BOOK OF CLEAR LIGHT

Copies of a manuscript called *Sefer HaBahir*, attributed to Nechunya ben ha-Kanah, a second century rabbinic figure, began to circulate in Provence France toward the end of the 12th century. This volume is a collection of homilies and commentaries on biblical verses. Still considered part of the so-called *Merkavah* tradition, it was likely edited in the late twelfth century.

Sefer HaBahir introduced a new conception of God. No longer was God the transcendent Sovereign of *Merkavah* mysticism. In *Sefer HaBahir* God is conceived as a blend of dynamic powers always in a state of ebb and flow.

The prime importance of *Sefer HaBahir* lies in its use of symbolic language. It is the earliest source that deals with the realm of the divine attributes (*sefirot*). It interprets a large part of the Bible as being concerned with events in the divine realm and the action of God's attributes rather than what happened in the created world. The *sefirot*, first mentioned in the *Sefer Yetzirah* as corresponding to the ten basic numbers, became divine attributes, lights, and powers in *Sefer HaBahir*, each one of which fulfills a particular function in the work of creation. Everything in the lower world contains a reference to something in the world of divine attributes.

In Spanish kabbalistic circles *Sefer HaBahir* was accepted as an authoritative source, composed by the Talmudic mystical sages, which greatly influenced the development of their teaching.

ISAAC THE BLIND

Isaac the Blind is the first identifiable kabbalist in Jewish history. In Hebrew he was known euphemistically as Yitzchak Sagi Nahor (Isaac of the Great Light). Bachya ibn Asher (one of the most distinguished of the biblical exegetes of Spain) called him the "Father of Kabbalah." Considerable information about Isaac can be gleaned from traditions preserved among his disciples, as well as from is pamphlets and other fragments of his writings that have survived.

Fragments of his writings contain lengthy exegeses concerning the mysticism of lights and colors. According to testimonies of his followers, he was also purported to hold mystical powers including the revelation of Elijah the prophet and magical power in prayer.

The fragments of his writings about *kavanah* (concentration and intention) and various forms of meditation to be used in various prayers are founded on a complete system of the *sefirot*, the attributes of God. According to Isaac the Blind, there are three levels within the Divine: *Ein Sof* (the cause of thought), *Machshavah* (thought) and *Dibbur* (speech). *Ein Sof* is so mysterious (even in relation to Divine thought) that it cannot be conceived of through thought or the annihilation of thought. On the other hand, he deals with *Machshavah* (thought) at great length with regard to the first *sefirah*. For Isaac, every mystic aspires to unite and derive sustenance from the sphere of thought, which is the object of *kavanah* around which religious aspiration is centered. Thought is the revelation of the hidden God, called *Ayin* (nothingness). Nothingness symbolizes the higher existence of the Divine in its most hidden manifestation.

The world of *Dibbur* (speech) begins with the *sefirah* of *Chochmah*. Isaac often uses the words *devarim* (words) or *dibburim*" (speeches) as synonyms for the *sefirot*. This outlook views the development of the world as a linguistic one, the Creator's expression in His language. Isaac sees the materialization of the Divine Speech in all areas of creation. The apparent letters are nothing but a manifestation of the inner letters by which the Divine Words came into being, and they are the bases of the world.

The *sefirot* are not only attributes of God but are also the principles of the world outside the world of the *sefirot*, called the *olam ha-nifradim*, the world of the separables. There is a continuous stream of emanation from the Divine Transcendence to the world of the separables. Isaac's primary goal was to show the way to communicate with the world of the Divine attributes through contemplation, intention, and devotion, which he viewed as the secret of the whole Torah and of prayer.

Tzippiyah (contemplation) is the internal connection between all essences and stages of creation. All things contemplate one another and are connected with one another, and thus there exists a universal dialectical process of emanation and spreading out to the limit of lower existence on the one hand and contemplating upward (*teshuva* – repentance) on the other.

NACHMANIDES

All of the early disciples of Isaac the Blind believed that it was impossible to reach or understand God through rational means. God could only be understood through symbols and traces of God's existence that He had planted throughout the universe. They believed that everything is a symbol of God – the human soul, the Torah, nature – if one knows how to decipher its meaning.

The challenge of understanding the symbolism of God was picked up by the next generation of kabbalists, students of Isaac the Blind living in the town of Gerona in northern Spain. Moshe ben Nachman, also known as Nachmanides, was the acknowledged leader of the Gerona school. Many of his writings express his mystical views. This is especially evident in his commentary on the Torah, which contains many veiled and unexplained allusions to interpretations according to "the true way," meant to arouse the curiosity of readers who were unfamiliar with this view. He also employed kabbalistic symbolism in some of his *piyyutim* (liturgical poems), and many consider Nachmanides to be the first kabbalistic poet. Nachmanides devotion to the kabbalah contributed to the dissemination of Jewish mystical teachings throughout Spain, Italy, and Israel.

THE ZOHAR

The most decisive event in the history of Spanish kabbalah was the advent of the *Sefer HaZohar*, the Book of Splendor. The discovery of the *Zohar* in the late thirteenth century in Spain ushered in a new era in the history of Jewish mysticism.

The *Zohar*, meaning "radiance" or "splendor" became the kabbalists' principal text. Like the early *Midrash*, the *Zohar* is a symbolic and allegorical exegesis of the *Torah*. The homiletical, discursive style is prominent, and stories abound. According to tradition, the *Zohar* was composed in the second century CE by Rabbi Simeon ben Yochai, who supposedly hid in a cave for thirteen years to avoid Roman persecution. However, the many linguistic anachronisms in the work (it is written mainly in Aramaic) and its references to religious and social practices prove that it is basically a medieval composition which modern scholarship attributes to the Spanish sage and kabbalist Moses de Leon (1240–1305). Like other pseudepigraphic writers before him, Moses de Leon, attributed his text to a famous ancient personality in order to gain greater renown for his work. Moses de Leon's sources were various *midrashim*, the *Babylonian Talmud*, and the Aramaic translations of the *Bible*. He also drew on medieval works, including the philosophic texts of Maimonides and Judah HaLevi, and the kabbalistic writings of his own era.

During the several centuries following its composition, the *Zohar* ranked with the *Bible* and the *Talmud* as the leading texts of Judaism and was the first book since the *Talmud* to achieve canonical status. Within fifty years of its appearance, it had circulated widely among Jewish communities.

Like the Talmud the *Zohar* is not one book, but rather a vast compilation with many parts. In addition to the main section, which is arranged according to chapters of the *Torah*, there are twenty-three other divisions. Like the *Talmud* it lacks an organizing doctrine and is dependent upon free association. Thus, if a word or an idea triggers another similar phrase or thought, the discussion freely follows that tangent.

Although the *Zohar* uses the four traditional methods of exegesis (the literal, the *aggadic* or homiletic, the allegorical and the mystical), it is the mystical that is the most important for the *Zohar*. In line with the kabbalists' desire to find a means of drawing near to God and searching for perfect communion with God, the *Zohar* seeks to illumine the words of the *Torah* with a higher, more profound meaning, and to seek out the hidden nuances of words and phrases.

The *Zohar* focuses on topics such as the soul, the nature of God, the symbolic meaning of the Sabbath, and the origin of the universe. In a nutshell, its main theme is that our ordinary world on earth is only a reflection of a higher spiritual world in heaven. The lower world is patterned after the upper world in heaven. The *Zohar* furthermore asserts that every human action on earth calls for a corresponding action in heaven. Thus, if a person does kindness on earth, that person will help to awaken God's kindness above. Similarly, if a person does evil on this earth, God's anger will be aroused in heaven. When one observes God's commandments, one can bring about greater harmony between the upper and lower worlds. In contrast, when one transgresses, one causes a separation between the two worlds.

Printed editions of the *Zohar* are comprised of five volumes. In most editions, three of the divisions appear under the title *Sefer HaZohar al ha-Torah* (translation); one volume is entitled *Tikkunei ha-Zohar* (translation); and the fifth, *Zohar Chadash* is a collection of sayings and texts found in the manuscripts of the kabbalists of Safed after the printing of the *Zohar* and assembled by Abraham ben Eliezer ha-Levi Beruchim. In summary, the complete *Zohar* includes:

1. The main part of the *Zohar* is arranged according to the weekly *Torah* portions, up to and including the portion of *Pinchas*. The only portions included from the book of *Deuteronomy* are *Va-etchanan*, a small section on *Vayelech* and the portion of *Haazinu*. Basically, it is a kabbalistic *midrash* on the Torah, combined with short statements, long expositions, and narratives about Simeon ben Yochai and his companions. Each exposition is preceded by introductions (*petichot*) which are usually based on verses from the *Prophets* and

the *Writings*, especially the *Psalms*. For the most part, the Zohar is written in Aramaic.

2. *Zohar to the Song of Songs* consists of kabbalistic expositions of *Shir HaShirim*.

3. *Sifrei di'Tzeni'uta* (Book of Concealment) is a fragmented commentary on the portion of *Bereshit* (Genesis) written in short, obscure sentences. In five chapters, it appears at the end of the portion of Terumah.

4. *Idra Rabba* (The Greater Assembly) is a description of the gathering of Simeon ben Yochai and his companions, in which profound mysteries concerning the revelation of the Divine in the form of *Adam Kadmon* (Primordial Man) are expounded. It is the most systematic discourse found in the *Zohar* which appears in the portion of *Naso*.

5. *Idra Zuta* (The Lesser Assembly) is a description of the death of Simeon ben Yochai that includes his closing words to his followers prior to his death. This portion concludes the *Zohar*.

6. *Idra de-Vei Mashkena* is the transcript of a study session conducted by Simeon ben Yochai with some of his students that expounds on certain verses at the beginning of the portion of Terumah that deal with the tabernacle and the mysteries of prayers.

7. *Heichalot*, which is found at the end of the portion *Pekudei*, includes two descriptions of the seven palaces in the heavenly garden of Eden where souls are believed to experience delight when prayer ascends after their departure from the world.

8. *Raza de-Razin* (The Secret of Secrets) is an anonymous piece on physiognomy and chiromancy, based on *Exodus* 18:21, in the portion of *Yitro*. Physiognomy is the art of determining people's character based on physical appearance. Chiromancy is the art of predicting a person's future by interpreting the lines on the palms of the hand.

9. *Sava de-Mishpatim* (Discourse of the Old Man) is an accounting of an encounter between Rabbi Yeiva, an old man and great kabbalist, and his companions. Rabbi Yeiva disguises himself as a donkey driver and delivers an extensive discourse on the theory of the

soul, based on the interpretation of the laws of slavery in the Torah. It is inserted as part of the body of the *Zohar* on the portion of *Mishpatim*.

10. *Yanuka* (The Child) is the story of a wonder child, the son of an old man named Rav Hamnuna, who teaches the companions profound interpretations of the Grace after Meals and other matters when they happen to be lodging in his mother's house. It is inserted in the portion of *Balak*.

11. *Rav Metivta* (Head of the Academy) is an account of a visionary journey undertaken by Simeon ben Yochai and his students to the Garden of Eden, and a long exposition by one of the heads of the celestial academy about the world to come and the mysteries of the soul. It appears as part of the portion *Shelach Lecha*.

12. *Kav ha-Middah* (The Standard of Measure) explains the details of the mysteries of emanation in an interpretation of the *Shema*, in the form of a discourse by Simeon by Yochai to his son that appears in *Zohar Chadash*.

13. *Sitrei Otiyot* (Secrets of the Letters) is a discourse by Simeon ben Yochai on the letters of the Divine Names and the mysteries of emanation that appears in *Zohar Chadash*.

14. A section without a title that appears in *Zohar Chadash* is an interpretation of the vision of the chariot in the first chapter of the *Book of Ezekiel*.

15. *Matnitin and Tosefta* contain a variety of short pieces that serve as a kind of *Mishneh* (explanatory addition) to the *Talmud* of the *Zohar* itself. Many of the pieces appear as utterances by a divine voice that is heard by the companions, urging them to open their hearts to an understanding of the mysteries. These pieces are scattered throughout the Zohar.

16. *Sitrei Torah* (Secrets of the Torah) are selections related to certain verses from the *Book of Genesis*, that appear in separate columns parallel to the main text of the *Zohar* in the portions of *Noah*, *Lech Lecha*, *Vayera* and *Vayetze*, and in the *Zohar Chadash* in the portions of *Toldot* and *Vayeshev*. It contains allegorical explanations of verses on the mysteries of the soul.

17. *Midrash ha-Ne'lam* (Concealed Midrash) centers on discussions of creation, the soul, and the world to come that pertain to the sections of *Bereshit, Noah,* and *Lech Lecha* in the *Zohar Chadash,* and for *Vayera, Chaye Sarah* and *Toldot* in the main body of the *Zohar. Midrash ha-Ne'lam* appears in *Zohar Chadash* in the portion of *Vayetze.* Most of the sections after the portion of *Bereshit* expound Bible narratives, notably the deeds of the patriarchs, as allegories on the fate of the soul.

18. *Midrash ha-Ne'lam to the Book of Ruth* appears in the *Zohar Chadash* and is similar in content to the concealed midrash described above.

19. *Midrash ha-Ne'lam to the Song of Songs* appears in the *Zohar Chadash* as a preface to the book.

20. *Ta Hazei* (Come and See) is another interpretation of the portion of *Bereshit* comprised of short anonymous comments found in Zohar Chadash.

21. *Ra'aya Meheimna* (The Faithful Shepherd) refers to Moses. This is a separate book on the kabbalistic significance of the commandments, found in some manuscripts as an independent work. In the printed editions its content is scattered among the sections in which the particular commandments are mentioned. The greater part appears in portions from *Numbers* and *Deuteronomy,* particularly in the portions of *Pinchas, Ekev* and *Ki Tetze.* In this book, Simeon ben Yochai and his companions meet the faithful shepherd (*i.e.,* Moses) in a vision, along with *tannaim* (rabbinic sages from 10–220 CE) and *amoraim* (rabbinic sages from 200–500 CE) and other celestial figures who talk to them about the mysteries of the commandments.

22. *Tikkunei Zohar* is an independent book, set in a context similar to the *Ra'aya Meheimna.* It is a commentary on the portion of *Bereshit,* with each section (*tikkun*) beginning with a new interpretation of the word *bereshit* (in the beginning). The book was designed to contain seventy *tikkunim,* conforming to the seventy aspects of the Torah. Among the points discussed are the mysteries of the vowel points and accents, mysteries concerning Jewish legal matters, and prayer.

23. Another untitled work on the portion of *Yitro which appears* in *Zohar Chadash*, is a redaction, in the spirit of the *tikkunim*, of the physiognomy found in the *Raza de Razin*.

STYLE AND SOURCES OF THE *ZOHAR*

The organized group of so-called "companions" (*chavraya*) contributes to the constructional unity of the *Zohar*. These companions are Simeon ben Yochai, his son Eleazar, Abbah, Judah, Yose, Isaac, Hezekiah, Chiya, Yeiva and Acha. These characters are joined by certain other rabbis, who usually appear indirectly, or as figures from the generation that proceeded Simeon ben Yochanan.

The Palestinian setting of the *Zohar* is fictitious. The *Zohar*, in the main, relies on geographical and topographical notions about Palestine that are taken from older literature, but some places that never existed are created. With regard to the characters, there are very close ties between the main body of the *Zohar* and the stratum of the *Midrash ha-Ne'lam*, which also mentions places that did not actually exist. In this section Simeon ben Yochai and his companions constitute the most important community of mystics, but other groups are mentioned as well.

Regarding the *Zohar's* sources, one must distinguish between several types. Fictitious works that are mentioned throughout the *Zohar* and *Midrash ha-Ne'lam* include: *Sifra de-Adam*, Sifre *de-Chanoch*, Sifra *di-Shelomo Malka*, Sifra *de-Rav Hamnuna Sava*, Sifra *de-Rav Yeiva Sava*, *Sifrei Kadma'ei* (ancient books), *Sifra de-Aggadeta*, the *Raza de-Razin* and the *Matnita di-Lan*. The *Atvan Gelifin* (engraved letters) is quoted regarding the mystery of the letters of the alphabet. Works of magic are also quoted, including *the Sifra de-Ashmedi*, the *Zeinei Charshi de-Kasdiel Kadma'ah* (various kinds of sorcery of the ancient Kasdiel), *the Sifra de Chochmeta di-Venei Kedem* (Book of wisdom of the sons of Kedem). The actual literary sources of the *Zohar* are concealed. These sources comprise a great many books, from the *Talmud* and *Midrashim* to the kabbalistic works that were composed in the 13th century. The main sources include: the *Babylonian Talmud*, Midrash *Rabbah*, Midrash *Tanchuma* and the two *Pesiktot*, the *Midrash on Psalms*, *Pirke de Rabbi Eliezer*, and Targum *Onkelos*. Some reference is also made to the *halachic midrashim*, the *Jerusalem Talmud*, and the other *Targums*. Other smaller *midrashim* include: *Heichalot Rabbati*, *Alphabet of Ben Sira*, *Sefer Zerubabel*, *Baraita de-Ma'aseh Bereshit*, *Aggadot Gan Eden* and *Sefer HaYashar*. Medieval Bible commentators such as Rashi, Ibn Ezra, Kimchi and the *Lekach Tov* of Tobiah ben Eliezer, and Nachmanides are also referenced.

An important exposition in the section of *Balak* is based on a combination of three pieces from the *Kuzari* (a story taking place during a conversion of some Khazar nobility to Judaism) of Judah HaLevi. Maimonides' commentary on the *Mishneh* and the *Guide to the Perplexed* (a theological work to find rational explanations for many events in the Bible) is also referenced.

SAMPLE TEXTS FROM THE *ZOHAR*

Following are several sample texts from the *Zohar* that deal with the primal divine light and the creation of man.

Primal Light

> *And God said: Let there be light, and there was light.*
> *(Genesis 1:3)*

This is the original light which God created the light of the eye. It is the light which God showed to Adam, enabling him to be able to see from one end of the world to the other end. It was also the light which God showed to David, who upon seeing it, burst forth into praise, saying: "How abundant is your goodness which You have laid up for them ⸺ You" (*Psalm 31:20*).

⸺ read ⸺ ght through which God showed to Moses the land of Isr⸺ors wc ⸺ to Dan. When God foresaw that three generations of the fl⸺ uld arise, namely the generation of Enosh, the ⸺ od, and the generation of the Tower of Babel,

God put the light away so that they should not enjoy it and gave it to Moses for the first three months of his life, while his mother hid him. When Moses was brought before Pharaoh, God withdrew the light from him, and only restored it to him when he stood on Mount Sinai to receive the Torah. From that time on, Moses had use of the light for the rest of his life, so that the Israelites could not approach him until he put a veil over his face (*Exodus 34:30*).

Let there be light, and there was light. (Genesis 1:3)

In Kabbalah, the term *vayhi* (and there was) is applied to anything that is found in this world and the next world. According to Rabbi Isaac: Luria "The radiance which God produced at the time of the creation illumined the world from one end to the other, but was retracted, in order that the world's transgressors might not enjoy it, and it is treasured up for the righteous (*i.e.*, for the *Tzadik*), as it is written, "light is sown for the *tzaddik*" (*Psalm 97:11*).

Until the time when the future world emerges and be firmly established, this light is concealed and stored up. The light issued from the darkness was carved out by the strokes of the most abstruse. Similarly, the lower world darkness in which light resides was carved out from that light which was stored away there by a hidden process. The lower darkness is what is called "night" in the verse "and the darkness he called night" (*Genesis 1:5*).

Creation of Man

God formed man of the dust of the ground and breathed into his nostrils the breath of life. (Genesis 2:7)

Rabbi Simeon arose and spoke: "My meditation disclosed to me that when God came to create man, all creatures trembled above and below. The sixth day was proceeding on its course wh▉▉▉ length the divine decision was formed. Then the source of all l▉▉▉ one forth and opened the gate of the East, for thence ligh▉▉▉ ▉e South displayed in full power the light which it ha▉ ▉m the ▉ginning and joined hands with the east. The▉ ▉f the

North, and the North awakened and spread forth and called aloud the West to come and join in. Then the West went up into the North and united with it, and afterwards the South took hold of the West, and the South and the North, which are the fences of the Garden, surrounded it. Then the East approached the West, and the West was rejoined and said to the others, 'Let us make man in our image, after our likeness,' embracing like us the four quarters and the higher and the lower. Then the East united with the West and produced him. Thus, our sages have said that man emerged from the site of the Temple. Further, the words 'let us make man' may be taken to signify that God imparted to the lower beings who came from the side of the upper world the secret of forming the divine name 'Adam,' which embraces the upper and the lower in virtue of its three letters, *alef, dalet and final mem*. When these three letters descended below, together in their complete form, the name Adam was found to comprise male and female. The female was attached to the side of the male until God cast him into a deep slumber, during which he lay on the site of the Temple. God then sawed her off from him and adorned her like a bride and brought her to him, as it is written, 'And he took one of his sides and closed up the place with flesh' (*Genesis 2:21*).

I have found it stated in an old book that the word 'one' here means 'one woman,' to wit, the original Lilith, who was with him and who conceived from him. Up until that time, however, she was not some help to him, as it is written, 'but for Adam there was not found a help meet for him.' Observe that Adam came last of all, it being fitting that he should find the world complete on his appearance."

No plant of the field was yet in the earth (Genesis 2:5)

Simeon said further: "These are the great trees which were planted out later yet were tiny. We have stated that Adam and Eve were created side by side. Why were they not created face to face? Because 'God had not yet caused it to rain on the earth' (*Genesis 2:5*), and the union of heaven and earth was not yet firmly established. When the lower union was perfected and Adam and Eve were turned face to face, then the upper union was fulfilled. We know this from the case of the tabernacle, of which we have learned that another tabernacle was erected with it, and that the upper one was not raised till the lower one was raised. And similarly, here. Further, since all was not yet in order above, Adam and Eve were not created face to face. The order of verses in the Bible proves this. For first we read, 'For God has not caused it to rain upon the earth,' and then 'there was not a man to till the ground,' the meaning being that man was still defective, and only when Eve was perfected was he also perfected. Next, a mist went up from the ground, to repair the deficiency below, by 'watering the whole face of the ground.' The rising of the mist signifies the yearning of the female for the male. According to another explanation, we supply the word 'not' from the previous clause after 'mist,' the meaning being that God did not send rain because a mist had not gone up, it being necessary for the impulse from below to set in motion the power above. So, vapor first ascends from the earth to form the cloud. Similarly, the smoke of the sacrifice rises and creates harmony above, so that all unite, and in this way, there is completion in the supernal realm. The impulse commences from below, and from this all is perfected. If the community of Israel did not give the first impulse, the One above would not move to meet her, for by the yearning from below completion is effected above."

The Serpent and Satan

> *Now the serpent was more subtle than any beast of the field which the Lord God had made. (Genesis 3:1)*

Rabbi Isaac said: "This is the evil tempter." Rabbi Judah said that it means literally a serpent. They consulted Rabbi Simeon and he said to them: "Both are correct. it was Samael, and he appeared on a serpent, for the ideal form of the serpent is the Satan. We have learned that at that moment Samael came down from heaven riding on this serpent, all creatures saw his form and ran away. They then entered a conversation with the woman, and the two brought death into the world. Of a surety Samael brought curses on the world through Wisdom and destroyed the first tree that God had created in the world. This responsibility rested on Samael until another holy tree came, namely Jacob who wrested the blessings from him, in order that Samael might not be blessed above and Esau below. For Jacob was the reproduction of Adam, and he had the same beauty as Adam. Therefore, as Samael withheld blessings from the first tree, so Jacob, who was such another tree as Adam, withheld blessings, both upper and lower from Samael. And in doing so Jacob took back his own. It is written that the serpent was subtle. This serpent is the evil tempter and the angel of death. It is because the serpent is the angel of death that it brought death to the world.

GOD AND THE *SEFIROT*

Jewish mystics think very deeply about how a person could and should imagine God. Their approach is that human beings cannot know what God is, but they can understand the powers that God used to create and sustain the universe and govern the people itself.

According to mystical thought, God neither has a name nor an attribute, and nothing can be said about God except that God exists. In Jewish mysticism this absolute divinity is called *Ein Sof* (The Infinite) and God's mysterious powers are known as *sefirot* (emanations of God).

The term *Ein Sof* means infinite and without end. For the kabbalists, God is not limited by space, has no physical form, and God's being extends without end. God is everywhere, and God is greater than the entire universe. God is also eternal and thus can never be limited to time. Because God is infinite, what God really is cannot be imagined by humankind. Since the reality of God really must always remain a mystery, the mystics speak of this aspect as "the hidden God."

In thinking about how God created the world and humankind, the kabbalists posited the existence of *sefirot*, divine luminaries or spheres through which God is revealed. The word *sefirot* comes from the Hebrew word *sappir* (sapphire) because the mystics compare the brightness of God to that of a sapphire gem. They think of the *sefirot* as spheres of very bright light that God sent forth when creating the world. Through these *sefirot*, say the kabbalists, the world came into being and is preserved. There were ten *sefirot* that God used in creating the world. Their names are *keter* (crown), *chochmah* (wisdom), *binah* (understanding), *chesed* (mercy), *din or gevurah* (judgment or power), *tiferet* (beauty), *netzach* (eternity), *hod* (majesty), *yesod* (foundation) and *malchut* (kingdom). The ten *sefirot* form a hierarchy: *keter*, the highest of the *sefirot*, is the closest to the *Ein Sof*.

The first three *sefirot* stand for the powers of God's mind, which God used to plan the creation of the world.

> *Keter* refers to the will of God. Thus, when beginning to create the world, God's first step was to exert the will to create.
>
> Similarly, after God willed the creation of the world, God thought about all the possible ways to bring the world into existence. Thus, the name for God's thought or wisdom was the second *sefirah* – *chochmah* (wisdom).
>
> Next, God decided on a specific plan as the best choice of action for creating the world. The name for God's understanding was the third *sefirah* – *binah*.

To visualize the balance between *chochmah* and *binah* in God, Jewish mystics see these two *sefirot* as flowing from *Keter*.

Having created the world, God needed principles by which to govern it. The middle three *sefirot* stand for the moral principles that God uses to rule the world.

> The fourth *sefirah*, *chesed* (God's mercy or kindness) was balanced by *din* (judgment), the fifth *sefirah*.
>
> A sixth *sefirah*, *tiferet* (beauty) was required to create the necessary harmony between mercy and judgment,

It became apparent to the mystics that the *sefirot* of mercy and judgment are not always balanced. When the sins of people exceed their good deeds, *din* (God's judgment) is no longer balanced with *chesed* (kindness). This is one reason that evil comes into the world. But when the good deeds outweigh the sins of people, there is harmony in heaven, represented by *tiferet*.

The third group of *sefirot* stand for God's principles of ruling the natural, physical world. The mystics believed that God's powers had both male and female aspects. The male aspect was represented on the right side of the *sefirot*, and the female on the left.

> The seventh *sefirah*, *netzach* (eternity) stands for the male aspect of God's powers, and it represents the power of nature to increase itself.
>
> The eighth *sefirah*, *hod* (majesty) stands for the limiting aspect of nature, always keeping a check on the *sefirah* of *netzach*.
>
> The ninth *sefirah*, balancing *netzach* and *hod*, represents the harmony of nature. It is called *yesod* (foundation) and represents the balance of nature.

The kabbalists believed that God's love for the Jewish people was so great that God wished to reveal His presence to them. Often comparing God's love for Israel to the love of a king or queen, the tenth and final *sefirah* – *malchut* – represents the union of God, the King, with His queen (the people of Israel). This *sefirah* is also known as the *Shechinah* – God's presence. The union of God with Israel is the climax of creation.

Mystics believe that they connect themselves with God's creative powers and God's actual Presence as it "poured forth" in creation by meditating on the *sefirot*. Human beings are a microcosm of the universe that unite the "upper" and "lower" worlds. For mystics who know how to interpret the symbolic language of outer reality, traces of God, embodied in the *sefirot*, are found in everything and discernible in everything, Thus, God not only revealed Himself at Mount Sinai, but in everything since the beginning of the creation and will continue to reveal Himself at the end of time.

The *Shechinah* in Kabbalah

The Hebrew word *Shechinah* (literally "dwelling" or "resting") refers to the Divine Presence of God in rabbinic literature. It is used to express the immanence and the omnipresence of God. We are told that the *Shechinah* is where people gather for worship, where judges sit as a court, and where even one person studies *Torah* (*Talmud, Berachot 6a*).

The basic elements of the kabbalistic concept of the *Shechinah* are found in the *Sefer Ha-Bahir*, the early mystical work in which the *Shechinah* (alternately called *Malchut* or kingdom), is described as the daughter and feminine principle in the world of the divine *Sefirot*. The *Shechinah* is the tenth and last in the hierarchy of the *Sefirot*. In the divine world it represents the feminine principle. All the elements and characteristics of the other *sefirot* are represented within the *Shechinah*. Like the moon, she has no light of her own, but receives divine light from the other nine *sefirot*.

The main goal of the realm of the *sefirot* is to restore the true unity of God – the union of the masculine principle (*Tiferet*) and the *Shechinah*, which was originally undisturbed but was broken by the transgressions of the people of Israel. The restoration to the state of original harmony can be affected by the religious acts of the Jewish people (*i.e.*, keeping the commandments and worshipping God).

The symbolism describing the *Shechinah* is the most developed in mystical literature. Most of the varied symbols refer to aspects of the *Shechinah's* relationship with the other *sefirot* above her – such as her acceptance of the divine light from them, her relationship to them as a lower aspect of themselves which is nearer to the created world, and her coming close to the masculine element or moving further away from it.

In another symbolic representation, the *Shechinah* is the battleground between the divine powers of good and evil. Because of her femininity and closeness to the created world, the *Shechinah* is the first and the primary target of satanic power. It is thus the duty of human beings and the *sefirot* to protect the *Shechinah* from these evil powers.

The *Shechinah* is considered the divine power that is closest to the created world, its source and its sustaining power. The divine light which maintains the created world passes through the *Shechinah*. The angels and the world of the *Merkavah* are all her servants.

In kabbalistic theology, the *Shechinah* is the divine principle of the people of Israel. Everything that happens to Israel in the earthly world is reflected by the *Shechinah*, who waxes and wanes with each good deed and every sin of each individual Jew. At the same time, everything that happens to the *Shechinah* in her relationship to the other *sefirot* and her battle against evil powers is reflected in the status of Israel in the earthly world. Furthermore. studying Torah and praying bring a Jew closer to the *Shechinah*, for she is symbolized as the *Oral Law*.

According to Kabbalistic understanding, the *Shechinah* is the divine power that is related to the prophets. Connecting with the *Shechinah* is also the first goal of the mystic, who tries to achieve *devekut* (communion) with the divine powers.

ABULAFIA'S "PATHS OF THE NAMES"

Abraham Abulafia was one of the most noteworthy of the thirteenth century mystics. He believed that contemplating the *sefirot* was only a prelude to a higher type of meditation, which he called "the Path of the Names." This practice consisted of meditating and reflecting on the names of God.

God has numerous names in Jewish tradition. The holiest name for God is the *Tetragrammaton*, a Greek word meaning "the name of four letters." The four Hebrew letters of the holiest name of God are *yud, hei, vav, hei,* often referred to in English as YHVH. The original pronunciation of this name of God was always considered to be too holy to be uttered by anyone except for the High Priest. Therefore, accepted Jewish practice is to pronounce the *Tetragrammaton,* as *Adonai,* meaning the Lord.

Abulafia believed that meditating on God's holiest name would lead to understanding the mystery of God. According to Abulafia, what a person could perceive with the five senses was not the only true reality. If a person could go beyond the five senses, he/she could know themselves as part of the One. Abulafia asserted that by meditating one could reach a new level of consciousness and experience the power of God.

Stage one of Abulafia's meditation focused on the letters of the Hebrew alphabet. He called his method *chochmat hatzeruf,* the science of combining letters. There are many Jewish legends about Hebrew letters. In one legend the Hebrew letters exist independently of ink and paper. In this legend Rabbi Chananya ben Teradyon was wrapped in a Torah scroll and burned at the stake. Just before his death, his students cried out: "Master, what do you see?" He responded: "The parchment is burning but the letters are flying toward the heavens" (*Talmud Avodah Zarah 8a*). This legend clearly reflects Abulafia's belief that meditation and reflection on Hebrew letters leads to knowledge of God.

Abulafia meditated on the Hebrew letters in three ways. He uttered their sounds. This was called *mivta* (articulation). He wrote the letters. This stage was called *michtav* (writing). And he thought about the letters. This stage was called *machshav* (thought).

By meditating on the Hebrew letters, he prepared himself for the highest stage, the meditation on God's holy name.

As a result of meditating on God's Name, Abulafia experienced a strange vision in which he saw himself speaking to himself and predicting the future. The vision connected the secret of God's holy name with Abulafia's hidden self, suggesting that if we truly understand ourselves, we can also possibly understand something about God.

Mysticism and Isaac Luria

Kabbalah draws on the mystic's awareness of both the transcendence and the immanence of God found in true religious life, every facet of which is a revelation of God. Theosophy seeks to reveal the hidden life of God and the relationships between the Divine life, on the one hand, and the life of humankind and creation, on the other.

By the Middle Ages mysticism had spread to Spain, France, and Germany. During the eleventh century it assumed a new dimension. No longer was mysticism only an approach to Torah study, but it also became a way of life for groups of learned and pious Jews who practiced meditation and contemplated the deep mysteries of Jewish prayer. All these acts were ways to attain spiritual serenity and communion with God.

In 1492 the Jews were expelled from Spain, and the once great center of Jewish learning was in ruins. In the wake of the spiritual and physical upheaval, many Jews migrated to the Middle East. A number of them settled in the Upper Galilee, drawn to the town of Safed, where a group of Jewish mystics set the stage for numerous mystical movements that emerged in the following 400 years, including a resurgence of interest in the study of kabbalah. Rabbi Isaac Luria, often referred to as Ha-Ari (the Lion) from the Hebrew initials of his title **Ha**Elohi **R**abbi **Y**itzchak (The divine Rabbi Isaac), was among the leaders of that community. He developed a new system for understanding the mysteries of the Zohar. It became known as the Lurianic method and shed new light on the hidden wisdom of the kabbalah.

Isaac Luria was born in Jerusalem in 1534, the son of German parents. His father died when he was still a child, and Luria was raised by his uncle Mordecai Francis, who had him educated by the best Jewish teachers. Luria excelled as a diligent student of rabbinic literature.

In his early twenties Luria became enthralled with the study of the Zohar, which had recently been printed for the first time. Adopting the life of a hermit, he secluded himself for seven years, giving himself up entirely to meditation.

During that time, he became a visionary, asserting that while asleep his soul ascended to heaven and conversed with great teachers of the past.

In 1569 Luria went to Israel, where he settled in Safed after a short sojourn in Jerusalem. It was there that he attracted a circle of kabbalists to whom he imparted the doctrines by which he hoped to establish the moral system of the world on a new basis. His circle included Moses Cordovero, Solomon Alkabiz, Joseph Karo (author of the *Shulchan Aruch* – the *Code of Jewish Law*), and Chayim Vital. His circle of students gradually widened, and his followers came to see Luria as a miracle worker.

According to Lurianic scholars, he did not actually write anything. Rather, his disciple Chayim Vital collected his lecture notes and produced numerous works to disseminate Luria's kabbalistic system. Luria died in Safed in 1572. A synagogue in Safed named the Ha-Ari after him continues to be a popular tourist attraction.

LURIA'S KABBALISTIC GOD

Kabbalists maintain that God is unknowable to the human mind. They further believe that God is unlimited and infinite, often referring to God as the *Ein Sof* (the Infinite One).

The kabbalistic system teaches that God is manifested or revealed through intermediary agents called *sefirot* (divine luminaries) from which God emanated. Meditation, prayer, study, and contemplation are ways for kabbalists to gain knowledge about God and how God relates to the world.

LURIA'S THREE STAGES OF CREATION

One of Luria's great contributions to Jewish thought was his doctrine of the three stages of creation. According to this doctrine:

Stage 1 – *Tzimtzum* (contraction), Luria wondered how it was possible that there was space for anything to coexist with God since God is everywhere. This question led Luria to posit the doctrine of *tzimtzum*, which means withdrawal or retreat. According to Luria, God contracted Himself and withdrew in order for the world to exist. By this act of withdrawal, God made room for the world by retreating from a portion of His universe. By retreating, God gave the people freedom to exist on their own and to choose between good and evil. Why did God create a world in which evil was even a possibility? Why did God not create a world that was perfectly good? The next two parts of Luria's theory attempted to answer these questions.

Stage 2 – *Shevirat HaKelim* (breaking of the vessels): Luria used myths and symbols to explain his theory, and attempted to explain why God had allowed the terrible suffering and tragedy of exile from Spain that occurred in 1492. According to this myth, known as "the breaking of the vessels," there is a flaw in the world. The flaw came about after God withdrew to allow space for creation of the world. God had created and destroyed many worlds. God destroyed these first worlds because the light emanating from God was too strong and powerful for people. These first worlds were called "vessels' and the destruction of these worlds was called "the breaking of the vessels." This cosmic catastrophe preceded the creation of our world.

In Luria's view, the world is flawed and imperfect as a result of the broken fragments of these vessels that have fallen into our world. These broken vessels, called *kelippot* (shells), are symbolic of evil. Evil breaks the order of the world, and everything in the world becomes a series of broken fragments. The exile of the Jews from Spain was compared to the broken fragments, moving the Jewish people from their place.

Stage 3 – *Tikkun* (repair of the world): Luria believed that God intended the world to be good. However, since human beings had free choice, evil was a possibility, which is why God allowed the breaking of the vessels to occur. God also gave human beings the power to combat evil. Sparks of light are symbolic of God's presence, and Luria believed that sparks of God's presence existed in the world. However, these Divine sparks were imprisoned in the *kelippot*, the broken fragments of the vessels. According to Luria, freeing these scattered sparks from their shells and reuniting them with God is the task of the Jewish people.

This myth thus gave purpose to the suffering of the exiled Spanish Jews. The exile came about to extract the last sparks of godliness in order to locate the good within the world. By searching for God, human beings can restore and repair the world to its original state of peace and harmony. The process of mending the world is called *tikkun*. Mending the world is accomplished through performance of *mitzvot* – God's commandments, as well as through prayer. Luria felt that true prayer, rendered with proper concentration and intention, would allow a person's soul to ascend and commune with God. The coming of the Messiah is the sign that complete *tikkun* has occurred.

LURIA'S FIVE SOULS

According to Luria, the *sefirot* were transformed into five "figures." The first *sefira, keter* (crown), was transformed into the three headed Macroprosopus (Creator of the Great World); the second *sefira, chochmah* (wisdom), was transformed into the active masculine principle called "Father"; the third *sefira, binah* (wisdom), became the passive, feminine principle called "Mother"; the six broken *sefirot* were transformed into the male child, which is the product of the masculine active and the feminine passive principles; the tenth *sefira, malchut* (kingdom), was transformed into the female child. According to Lurianic kabbalah, this transformation was absolutely necessary because if God had created these figures in the beginning instead of the *sefirot*, there would have been no evil in the world, and consequently no reward and punishment. The broken *sefirot* or vessels are the source of evil whereas the light of the *Ein Sof* produces only good.

These figures are found in each of Luria's five worlds: World of Emanation, World of Creation, World of Formation, and World of Action (which represents the material world). Above all this is the primordial world of initial consciousness.

Luria asserts that five souls emanate from the five fives. Ranked from highest to lowest they are: *neshamah, ru'ach, nefesh, chaya* and *yechidah*, and that the soul is the connecting link between the infinite and the finite. According to Luria, all of the souls destined for the human race were created from various organs of Adam. Each human soul is thus a spark from Adam. Adam's first sin caused confusion among the various classes of souls. The superior intermingled with the inferior, so that even the purest soul received a mixture of evil, or as Luria calls it, of the element of the *kelippot* (shells). The pagan world descended from the lowest classes of souls, while the Israelite world emanated from the highest classes. In this view, the state of confusion among souls will cease with the arrival of the Messiah who will establish the new moral system upon which the world will be based. Until that time, human beings' souls must wander through the bodies of animals, humans, and inanimate things such as stone and wood.

Luria said that every person bears on his or her forehead a mark that indicates the nature of his soul, to which degree and class it belongs, the wanderings it has already accomplished, and to which soul it should be united in order to become fully purified. This union can be affected by formulas of conjuration. (i.e., using magic spells and incantations).

CONCLUSION

For mystics, God exists but is unknowable, unlimited, and infinite. The ten *sefirot* provide the necessary bridge between the unknowable God and the known universe. Isaac Luria preferred a world where human beings were free to choose, even if this meant the possibility of evil. Luria's theory of God's contraction allows room for physical things in the world.

Luria also introduced his mystic system into religious observances.

For him, every commandment had a mystical meaning. He conceived of the Sabbath itself, with all its ceremonies, as the embodiment of the Divinity in temporal life. Every ceremony performed on the holy Sabbath was believed to have an influence on the superior world.

Finally, according to Luria, the mission of the Jewish people is to help mend the world through performance of God's commandments in order to gather the Divine sparks that have been scattered throughout the universe. In this view, the complete repair of the world will hasten the coming of the Messiah.

Mystical False Messiahs

Originally, the term *mashiach* (messiah) was applied to any person anointed with holy oil and consecrated to carry out God's purposes, such as the high priest or the king. When David received the divine promise that the throne would remain in his family forever (*Samuel* 11 7:13), the title acquired a special reference and signified the representative of the royal line of David. The prophetic vision of the eventual establishment of the divine kingship on earth came to be identified with the restoration of Israel under the leadership of the Messiah, God's anointed one.

Today Judaism's traditional outlook is that the Messiah will be the dominating figure of an age of universal peace and plenty. Jewish prayers are replete with references to messianic hopes and aspirations. Nearly all prophets of note mention the messiah and the messianic age.

KABBALAH AND THE AGE OF THE MESSIAH

The question has arisen: Why was the Zohar concealed from earlier generations, since they were undoubtedly at a more spiritual level and better able to understand the kabbalah's profound wisdom?

A clue to this quandary is provided in the Zohar itself, in a discourse on the coming of the Messiah:

> Rabbi Shimon raised his hands and wept and said, "Woe to him who meets with that period; praiseworthy is the portion of him who encounters and has the divine capacity to be cast with that time."

Rabbi Shimon then explains this paradoxical comment as follows:

> "Woe to him who meets with that period, for when the Almighty
> shall remember the Divine Presence, if God shall gaze upon those
> who stand loyal to God, upon all who are found in God's midst,
> and find among them a single righteous one, as the Bible warns,
> 'I looked, and there was none to help.' Agonizing torment and
> trouble lie in wait for Israel. Praiseworthy, however, are those who
> shall merit the joy-giving light of the King. Concerning that time,
> it is proclaimed: 'I will refine them as silver is refined, I shall try
> them as gold is tried.'" (*Zohar II, 7b*)

In this excerpt, Rabbi Shimon confirmed that the messianic era will
bring with it a light and richness representing the infusion of divine
purity through all the world. The dawn of a new world will appear,
and with its advent, the light will begin to liberate people from their
ignorance, bringing them a spiritual and intellectual awakening.

The *Zohar* also states that in the days of the Messiah, "there will
no longer be the necessity for one to request of his neighbor, 'teach
me wisdom,' as it is written, 'one day they will no longer teach every
man his neighbor, and every man his brother, saying " Know God,
for they shall all know Me, from the youngest to the oldest of them."
(*Zohar III, 58a*)

The *Zohar* expresses the idea that the Messianic era will usher in
a period of unprecedented enlightenment. Messianism, representing
the essence of hope and optimism, grows out of the belief that there
will be an eventual triumph of world harmony over confusion, of love
over hate, an ultimate victory of justice and kindness over oppression
and greed. This victory declares the *Zohar* is bound to *chochmah* (wisdom), and dependent upon the dissemination of true knowledge.

Whereas earlier generations were considered closer to the source
of spirituality than later ones, they demanded far less from the physical
world. They were on a higher physical and spiritual plane of existence
and could maintain their elevated status. Later generations had to rely
to a great extent on knowledge from secondary sources, such as the
written word. At the same time, later generations' greater dependence

on the world and their desire to receive makes them more capable of receiving the light.

FALSE MESSIAHS: ABRAHAM ABULAFIA

Numerous false messiahs have appeared throughout Jewish history. They claimed divinity or semi-divinity and were often killed or excommunicated by the community. The period of the false messiahs began in the thirteenth century with the kabbalist Abraham Abulafia. As a result of his mystical studies, Abulafia came to believe that he was a prophet. He declared that God had spoken to him in a book that he published in Urbino in 1279., He officially declared himself to be the Messiah in Messina on the island of Sicily where he had attracted many students and announced that the messianic era would begin in the year 1290. He was condemned by the medieval rabbi and Talmudist Solomon ben Adret (leader of Spanish Jewry in the 13th century) to whom the community appealed regarding Abulafia's claims. Persecuted in Sicily, he escaped to the island of Comino near Malta, still asserting his messianic mission in his writings. His end is unknown. Two of his students, Joseph Gikatilla and Samuel later claimed to be prophets and miracle workers as well.

NISSIM BEN ABRAHAM

Nissim ben Abraham was another false prophet who claimed to be the Messiah. Active in Avila, he claimed that he was advised by his followers that an angel had suddenly endowed him with the power to write a mystical work entitled *The Wonders of Wisdom*. The community once again appealed to Solomon ben Adret, who doubted Nissim's prophetic pretensions. Nissim ben Abraham continued his messianic activity and predicted that the date of the coming of the Messiah would be the last day of *Tammuz* in the year 1295. Those who believed in him prepared for the event by fasting and donating alms. When they convened on the appointed day instead of finding the Messiah, some saw little crosses pinned on their garments, perhaps placed there by unbelievers to ridicule the movement. Some of Nissim's followers were said to have converted to Christianity in disappointment, and what became of the false Messiah Nissim is unknown.

ASHER LEMMLEIN

A century later in 1502, Asher Lemmlein, a German, appeared in Istria near Venice, proclaiming himself to be the Messiah, He announced the Messiah would come within half a year if the Jews would repent and practice charity, and a pillar of cloud and smoke would precede the Jews on their return to Jerusalem. He found believers in Italy and Germany, even among the Christians. In obedience to his preaching, people fasted, prayed, and donated alms in preparation for the coming of the Messiah incompliance with his preaching.

The year came to be known as the "year of penitence. "When his prophecy proved false, Lemmlein either died or disappeared.

SOLOMON MOLKO

This kabbalist and false messiah was born of Marrano parents in Portugal. He was originally called Diogu Pieres. In 1525 he circumcised himself and took a Hebrew name (Molko is derived from *melech* meaning king).

He later settled for a period in Salonika, where he studied kabbalah and gathered many students who prevailed upon him to publish a collection of his sermons which are filled with the expectation of the coming redemption. His sermons attacked many people, including Christians. The accusations by an informer that he was a Marrano who had reverted to Judaism caused him to flee to Pesaro and eventually to Rome. By then Molko had become convinced that he indeed was the Messiah. In fulfillment of the Talmudic legend (*Sanhedrin 98a*) that recounted the suffering of the Messiah, Molko dressed as a beggar, sat among the sick and the infirm on a bridge over the Tiber near the Pope's palace for thirty days, tasting no meat or wine.

Molko succeeded in gaining the confidence of Pope Clement VII, who granted him protection in 1530. His standing was further strengthened when his prophecies of a flood in Rome (1530) and an earthquake in Portugal (1531) came true.

In 1530 Molko left for Rome, where he was accused of Judaizing and was condemned to be burned at the stake. He was saved by the personal intervention of the Pope. In 1532 Molko was tried and burned at the stake after refusing to recant and convert to Christianity.

ISAAC LURIA AND HAYIM VITAL CALABRESE

Both Isaac Luria and Hayim Vital Calabrese claimed to be Ephyraitic messiahs, forerunners of the Davidic messiah. These Jewish messiahs, known in Hebrew as Mashiach ben Yosef as well as Mashiach ben Ephraim, were said to be descendants from the tribe of Ephraim and a descendant of Joseph. In his mystic system Luria taught about the transmigration and superfetation of souls. Superfetation is the occurrence of a second conception during pregnancy, giving rise to embryos of different ages in the uterus. Transmigration is the passing of a soul from one body to another after death. Luria believed that he possessed the soul of the Messiah of the house of Joseph whose mission was to hasten the coming of the Messiah of the house of David through the mystic improvement of souls.

In 1569 he went to Safed in northern Israel, where he met Hayim Vital Calabrese, to whom he revealed his secrets and through whom he attracted many students. He secretly taught his messiahship to these adherents. He believed that the messianic era would commence in the beginning of the second half of the second day (of the year 1000) after the destruction of the Temple (i.e., in 1568).

Upon Luria's death, Hayim Vital Calabrese claimed to be the Ephraitic messiah and preached that the messianic era was soon at hand. According to tradition, Calabrese fell seriously ill in Safed in 1587, and upon recovering, he moved to Damascus where he remained until his death.

SHABBETAI ZEVI

Shabbetai Zevi was the most notorious of all false Messiahs. Shabbateanism, the messianic movement that was named after him, was the largest and most momentous messianic movement in Jewish history after the destruction of the Temple and the Bar Kochba revolt.

In 1665, half or more of world Jewry believed that Shabbetai Zevi, a Turkish Jew, was the Messiah who would soon free Palestine from Turkish rule and restore it as an independent Jewish state. In Germany upper-class Jews packed huge barrels of food and clothing in preparation for the long journey to Palestine.

Masses of Jews and even some rabbinic scholars were swept along in the messianic frenzy of Shabbetai Zevi's messianic movement. Several factors contributed to his following. On the one hand, the general condition of the Jewish people in exile and their hopes for political and spiritual redemption provided fertile soil for the blossoming of a messianic movement aimed at ushering in redemption. In addition, the newly popularized Lurianic kabbalah posited an intimate bond between Jewish religious activities including performance of commandments and recitation of meditations and prayer combined with the messianic message created the allusion that the final redemption was just around the corner.

Part of the credit for the messianic frenzy of the time must go to Shabbetai's most capable publicist, Nathan of Gaza. He dispatched persuasively written communiques throughout the Jewish world predicting the imminent return of the Ten Lost Tribes, the overthrow of the Turkish sultan, and Shabbetai's triumphant reign thereafter as the Messiah. Widespread and often naive, religious piety made the message irresistible to large numbers of Jews. The Chmielnitzki pogroms, in which more than one hundred thousand Jews were murdered, also persuaded many Jews that the messianic age must indeed be imminent.

Instead of a return to Zion, there was a catastrophe. Instead of Shabbetai confronting the Turkish sultan with his demand for Palestine, the monarch ruled that he convert to Islam or be tortured to death.

Shortly thereafter, Shabbetai entered the palace of the sultan, donned a turban, and took on the Muslim name of Mehemet Effendi.

The shock to the Jewish community was overwhelming, and once again the Jews suffered the great disappointment of a failed Messiah. Jesus had become the father of Christianity, Bar Kochba had led the Jews into a disastrous revolt and now Shabbetai had become a Muslim.

Even after Shabbetai's conversion to Islam, his publicist Nathan continued to insist that he was the Messiah but that his messianic task mandated that he descend into the lower world of Islam to redeem its impure sparks. Thousands of Jews accepted Nathan's rather far-fetched explanation.

Most Jews stopped believing that Shabbetai was the Messiah when they heard about his conversion to Islam, but a Jewish group in Turkey called the Doemeh converted to Islam while continuing to believe that Shabbetai was the Messiah. Shabbetai Zevi died after his fiftieth birthday in 1676.

JACOB FRANK

The last of the Shabbetain messiahs was Jacob Frank, who claimed to be Shabbetai's successor. He organized a movement that asserted that Jewish laws were voided in the new messianic age. Frank even organized wife-swapping orgies, which quickly led to his ostracism and persecution by the organized Jewish community.

Having secured a following among Turkish and Wallachian Jews, Frank arrived in Podolia (area in the Ukraine) in 1755. where the Sabbetaians needed a leader. He revealed himself as the reincarnation of the soul of the self-proclaimed messiah Shabbetai Tzvi. In accordance with the Sabbetaian doctrine of the Deity, he stressed the idea of the holy king, who was at the same time the Messiah, and accordingly called himself *Santo Senor* (Holy Lord). His followers claimed he performed miracles, and they even prayed to him. His ultimate purpose, as well as that of his sect, was to uproot talmudic Judaism. He was forced to leave Podolia and his followers were persecuted.

Returning in 1759, he advised his followers to embrace Christianity, and about one thousand converted. He converted in Warsaw in 1759. Later his insincerity was exposed, and he was imprisoned as a heretic, even in prison remaining the head of this sect. Frank died in 1791. His funeral was organized as a glorious demonstration by hundreds of his believers.

MOSES LUZZATTO

Moses Hayim Luzzatto (1707–1747) also believed himself to be a Messiah. He had been initiated into kabbalah earlier. Self-deluded as a result of his occupation with the Zohar and influenced by the mystical atmosphere in which he lived, he believed that a divine spirit had given him an insight into its mysteries. He fancied himself to be destined to redeem Israel by means of *The Second Zohar* which he wrote. At first his kabbalah remained within a narrow circle of students. When the secret was finally revealed, Luzzatto was forced to take an oath that he would refrain from writing, publishing, and teaching his doctrines unless he went to Palestine. Nevertheless, he returned to his kabbalistic activity and was excommunicated several times. In 1744 he went to Palestine to engage in his mystical studies undisturbed, and to fill his messianic role. He died there in 1747.

CONCLUSION

Of all the traditions in Judaism, the kabbalah, holds the most exalted concept of human beings, who are responsible for mending and healing the world. It is therefore understandable that the kabbalah allowed belief in a supernatural messiah who had the mystical power to save the Jewish people to arise. Shabbetai Zevi offered hope to many Jews at a terrible time in their history. But when it became very clear that the answer to their problems did not lie in a Messiah, Jews looked for another kind of mystical leader. This kind of leadership will be described in the next chapter.

Hasidim and the Baal Shem Tov

At the end of the seventeenth century, Polish Jews were in a depressed state. Sabbatai Zevi's conversion to Islam had disillusioned many of them, and the slaughter of over 100,000 Jews by the Ukrainian Cossacks in the mid-1600s had a dampening effect.

The times demanded a new kind of leadership from a person with charisma who could lift the people's spirits. That person was Israel ben Eliezer, known as the *BeShT* (*Baal Shem Tov* or Master of the Good Name). Born and bred in the Ukraine, the Baal Shem Tov's luminous personality and profound influence are the topics of countless legends. His striking magnetism, intuitive insight, and religious temperament explain the extraordinary veneration with which he was surrounded once his doctrines became known. People began to attribute unrivalled spiritual authority and miraculous powers to him. His teachings transmitted orally from generation to generation, are the basis of the vast didactic Hasidic literature.

Hasidim has been described as a revolt against a one-sided expression of Judaism presented in cold and learned teachings, which were understood by only a minority within the Jewish community. Israel Baal Shem Tov taught that all are equal before God, the ignorant no less than the Talmudic scholars, and that prayerful devotion and humility are more acceptable in heaven than intellectual attainments. He sought communion with God in the woods and in the fields, emphasizing that life is a divine manifestation.

The Baal Shem Tov further stressed the qualities of optimism and cheerfulness, by teaching serving God by avoiding sadness as much as possible and not to yield to paralyzing grief. For him this was a fundamental Jewish principle. Instead, a person should always concentrate their thoughts on God.

The omnipresence and immanence of God is the keynote of all his teachings. He taught that all things are pervaded by the divine life, and nothing is void of God. Since God is present in every human thought and in all things, there is actual or potential good in all things. Above all, people should realize that the true lover of God is also a lover of people. Every *mitzvah* must be done with *hitlahavut* (enthusiasm). Mechanical and lifeless performance of good deeds has little value. All people, including transgressors, and evil doers, must be loved, since they too have sparks of divinity in them.

In the mid 1730s, Israel Baal Shem Tov revealed himself as a healer and leader. Many people were attracted by his magnetism and widespread reports of his miracles, and several Hasidic groups that had been formed earlier came under his leadership and teaching.

Israel Baal Shem Tov undertook journeys to effect cures, expel demons and evil spirits, and win influence. Prayer became his main ecstatic and mystical approach to God, and intellectual study and learning took a secondary place. In especially exciting moments he was able to reach a state of mystical exaltation called *aliyat neshamah* (the ascent of the soul).

Modelling the importance of charity, he gave a great deal, including helping to ransom captives and prisoners. He taught that devotional joy was the proper attitude of the Jew in every moment of his or her life and in prayer. His admirers always spoke about the fiery way in which he recited his own prayers.

Legends about the life of the Baal Shem Tov abound. Many of the stories about him have been retold in Martin Buber's *Tales of the Hasidim*.

PRINCIPAL TEACHINGS

Although the teachings of the Baal Shem Tov derive to some extent from kabbalah and kabbalistic terminology, the original content of his brand of Hasidism emphasizes personal existence and the salvation of the individual's soul. He forbade any attempt at magical activity designed to hasten the coming of the Messiah.

The Baal Shem Tov did not put his teachings into writing. In fact, he wrote no books. Twenty years after his death, his student Yaakov Yosef of Polonnoye wrote down his teachings.

A summary of these teachings follows:

- The principle of *devekut* (adhesion or communion) is at the core of his teaching. He demanded that people practice *devekut* in all their daily acts and social contacts. That is to say, one must worship God and cling to God not only when practicing religious acts and pious deeds, but also in all daily affairs, in business and in social contacts. This belief is linked with the previously discussed Lurianic doctrine of raising the holy sparks, although the Baal Shem Tov limits this concept to the salvation of the individual soul alone.
- The Baal Shem Tov never advocated withdrawal from worldly life. Rather, he emphasized the need to find joy in worshipping God.
- He also taught the prime importance of Torah study. He believed that learners open the divine worlds before them by contemplating the letters of the text being studied. This belief assumed that the letters of the Torah evolved and descended from a heavenly source. Therefore, one who studies properly (*i.e.*, by contemplating the letters), restores the outward forms of the letters to their spiritual prototypes, their divine source.

  Study for its own sake is intended to enable the learner to attach him or herself in holiness and purity to the letters, which will make a person wise and radiate true eternal life.
- For the Baal Shem Tov, prayer is one of the main means of worshipping God. Through prayer a person has the potential of reaching *devekut* (cleaving to God) and contact with the divine world. As with the study of Torah, prayer can lead to *devekut* through

concentration on the mystical meaning of the letters. However, the Baal Shem Tov acknowledged that prayer which directs a person to attain *devekut* can at times be interrupted by undesirable thoughts which were understood to be derived from a heavenly source as the result of cosmic processes generally associated with the doctrine of the fallen holy sparks in Lurianic kabbalah. Therefore, he taught that one who prays must learn to properly deal with such foreign thoughts. According to this belief, the spark is hidden in the sinful thought and aspires to rise and be redeemed. One who learns to suppress the foreign thought can help the spark return to its divine source.

• According to some, the Baal Shem Tov's teaching contains hints that extraneous thoughts are the final stage in the kabbalistic process of *atzilut* (emanation). They are conceived of and identified with the *kelippot* (shells/forces of evil) at the extremity of emanation.

THE *TZADIK*

In Hasidic teaching the *tzaddik* is a person whose spiritual qualities are greater than those of other human beings and who have achieved an extraordinarily high level of *devekut*. The *tzaddik* is often viewed as the living incarnation of the Torah by his disciples and adherents. To fulfill his destiny, the *tzaddik* must both observe the *mitzvah* of *devekut* while at the same time maintaining contact with the material world and its people. The *tzaddik* both influences society and is influenced by it. His stature can be lowered by sins of power and his sinful thoughts cause others to commit transgressions.

The *tzaddik's* main goal in life is to teach people to worship God by means of *devekut* and to cause sinners to repent. The *tzaddik* descends spiritually to the sinner, associates with him, and by his own ascent raises the sinner and restores him to goodness.

Belief in the power of the *tzaddik* became one of Hasidism's strongest yet most controversial ideas. Opponents of Hasidism charged that the *tzaddik* often enriched himself at the expense of his followers.

THE MAGGID OF MEZHIRECH

The Baal Shem Tov chose Rabbi Dov Aber of Mezhirech, a gifted preacher (*maggid*) as his successor. After the Baal Shem Tov's death in 1760 Rabbi Dov Baer became the new leader of the Hasidim. Within twelve years the *Maggid* succeeded in establishing a Hasidic network that spanned all Eastern Europe, assigning a Hassidic Rebbe (a *tzaddik*) to each community.

Dov Baer undertook a profound study of Kabbalah, adopting the Lurianic system and an ascetic way of life. He had a charismatic personality and was an eloquent preacher and teacher.

Dov Baer formulated the doctrine that provided Hasidism with a speculative-mystical system, introducing the concepts of Kabbalah and a specific pattern of organization. Some consider his activities to be the beginning of Hasidism as a movement.

In Dov Baer's later years, his views on the Divinity, as well as methods of leadership, aroused fierce opposition from rabbis who did not accept the Hassidic way. They opposed the ecstatic modes of Hasidic religious worship, changes in prayer ritual adopted from Lurianic liturgy, and innovations in ritual slaughter.

Dov Baer's Teachings

For Dov Baer, the essence and presence of God penetrates all existence and embodies everything. By means of inner reflection and contemplation, a person can develop a close and direct relationship with God. Since every person can achieve this direct contact with God according Dov Baer's view, the *tzaddik* loses his function as the intermediary between the Hasid and God.

For Dov Baer, the purpose of human beings' life is to abolish concrete cosmic reality and return to the mystical *Ayin* (Nothingness) which preceded creation (*i.e.*, "God created existence out of nothing, and God makes nothingness out of existence"). The soul descends from the heights to raise up the material existence through its spiritual exaltation and thus restores the unity which was disturbed by the work of creation.

With regard to the essence of prayer, Dov Baer rejects the emphasis on the personal nature of supplication and advocates an attitude of indifference toward the results of the act. For Dov Baer, the act of prayer is a psychological exercise in maximal concentration, a technique focused on the denial of the self. In the transfer from vocal prayer (speech) to prayer by thought, the human act is converted into divine speech.

Dov Baer also emphasizes the necessity of meticulous observance of *mitzvot*, and in areas of *halacha* and Jewish law, he inclined toward practicality.

Unlike Luria's conception of *tzimtzum* as God's contraction to make way for the world to be created, Dov Baer conceives of *tzimtzum* as an act of emanation. He does not interpret the "breaking of the vessels" as a catastrophe within the divine world, but rather sees its purpose as illumination.

SAINT MYSTICS

Many outstanding religious leaders kept Hasidism alive between the years of 1750 and 1800. Following the death of Dov Baer in 1772, Hasidic leaders distributed authority among themselves, often designating their sons or other close relatives as their successors. In this way they created hereditary dynasties, some of which continue to the present day. The prominence of the Hasidic movement can be attributed to a number of these Hasidic leaders who developed their own unique styles of teaching and interpretation. They were not only mystics, seeking the concealed presence of God, but they were also considered saints, whose lives were models of true piety. Each saint-mystic offered a unique path to God.

RABBI LEVI YITZCHAK

Rabbi Levi Yitzchak Ben Meir of Berdichev, one of the most famous personalities in the third generation of the hasidic movement, was among these saintly personalities Born into a distinguished rabbinic family, his father was a rabbi in Galicia. In 1776 Levi Yitzchak went to study under Dov Baer, the Maggid of Mezhirech, joining his intimate circle of students. In 1775 he moved to Berdichev where he served as rabbi until his death and earned great renown as rabbi, hasidic leader and scholar.

His teachings stressed the element of joy in Hasidism, the principle of *devekut* (adhesion to God), and the imperative of impassioned prayer to the point of *hitpashetut ha-gashmiyut* (abstraction from corporeality). Levi Yitzchak asserted that when a person prays fervently with all one's heart and soul his spirit delights because it is elevated from the material world so that only the spirit remains. For this reason, every Jew is enjoined to worship God with true devotion and ardent fervor.

An itinerant preacher, Levi Yitzchak would travel from place to place, introducing people to the joy of fulfilling the commandments and winning them over to Hasidism. In singing his prayers he addressed God in Yiddish.

Levi Yitzchak distinguished between two types of preachers: one who admonishes with good words and shows people their merit and the source of their soul, bringing out their superior qualities, and the other who admonishes with harsh words and subdues people. He felt that only preachers who admonish people gently will elevate their souls.

Rabbi Levi Yitzchak of Berdichev did not set forth a theory to explain Jewish suffering, as Isaac Luria did. Rather, he searched for meaning in his suffering through questioning. He believed that it was incumbent on every Jew to ask the question, and for every individual to personally search for meaning in order to find it for themselves. In fact, the question was more important than the answer for Levi Yitzchak.

RABBI NACHMAN OF BRATSLAV

Born in 1772, this mystic-saint was the great grandson of the Baal Shem Tov on his mother's side and the grandson of Nachman of Horodenka on his father's side. His mother Feige was known as one who possessed the holy spirit.

Rabbi Nachman formulated a theory on the messianic status of the soul (which he viewed as including both messiah the son of David and messiah the son of Joseph). He also claimed that the messiah was destined to be one of his own descendants. His extremely radical doctrine on the *tzaddik* (which always referred to himself) encompassed his role as the messiah.

Like other Hasidic groups, one of the most important institutions of Bratslav Hasidism was the pilgrimage to the *tzaddik*. Nachman, however, did not receive visits from his hasidim on every Sabbath and holy day as was the custom at the courts of other *tzaddikim*. Rather, he received visitors at three designated times: Rosh Hashanah, the Sabbath of Hanukkah and Shavuot. On Rosh Hashanah in particular, all Bratslav Hasidim were obligated to visit their *tzaddik* and to pray in his company. The gathering on Rosh Hashanah was renewed after Rabbi Nachman's death by Nathan in Uman and has continued to this day.

The custom of confession before the tzaddik became a major institution among the Bratslaver Hasidim. Confession served as an initiation rite. When a Hasid first came within the orbit of the *tzaddik*, he would enumerate his sins in the form of a confession as a sign that he was becoming a Hasid of his master., The *tzaddik* would respond by prescribing suitable ways to repent.

Rabbi Nachman's Teachings

Rabbi Nachman's teachings contain many innovations that cover a variety of fields. According to Nachman, *Ein Sof* (the Infinite One) created the world in order to reveal its mercy. For Nachman, divinity is inherent in everything, even in the realm of the evil *kelippot*. Thus, if a man is saturated in evil, he can easily find the Creator and repent, for anything that can be broken can also be repaired.

Nachman also asserts that *tzimtzum* (God's withdrawal) will only be achieved in the future. He elaborates that the *kelippot* came into being because of the "breaking of the vessels" and designates a separate sphere for their destructive activity.

For Rabbi Nachman, worshipping God in naivete with no crafty side thoughts is the main purpose and perfection of human beings, that only comes about by faith and through the practical mitzvot that are performed according to the Torah. Thus, Nachman expresses bitter opposition to the study of philosophy, instead presenting faith as one of the highest religious values.

Nachman's view of the *tzaddik* uniquely claims that there is only one true *tzaddik*, Nachman himself, who is destined to be the messiah. The great *tzaddik's* reflection on heretical questions may bring about the spiritual elevation of those who were formerly sunk in error. Nachman strongly emphasizes the obligation of confessing before the *tzaddik* and advocates praising him. Communication with the *tzaddik* thus advances the process of *tikkun* (repair) that Lurianic kabbalah demands of Jews.

Rabbi Nachman's general outlook on humanity and the world is rather gloomy. He believes that although human beings encounter many obstacles in their path in this world. he rejects despair and rather emphasizes faith, joy, melody, dance, constant self-criticism, and communication with the *tzaddik* as life's goals.

Rabbi Nachman lauds the use of the *niggun* (melody without words) and posits that a complete system of these melodies suited to the composite range of the universe exists.

Rabbi Nachman's Writings

Almost all the existing Bratslav literature was committed to writing by Nathan ben Naphtali Hertz Sternhartz, Nachman's student, who served as his scribe. Sternhartz joined Rabbi Nachman's small group of Hasidim early in 1803. The first volume of Nachman's theological teachings, *Likkutei Moharan* (Ostroy, 1806) was published during his lifetime. The second volume, entitled *Likkutei Moharan Tinyana* (Mogilev, 1811) appeared posthumously. The tales that Rabbi Nachman began to relate in his last years (beginning in 1806) are collected in *Sippurei Ma'asiyot* (Berdichev, 1815).

Today most of the Bratslav hasidim in Israel are concentrated in Jerusalem, especially in the Old City. There is also a center of Bratslav Hasidim in Bene Berak, near Tel Aviv.

Mystical Elements in Prayer and Liturgy

KABBALISTIC WAYS TO GOD

Mystics have often sought to achieve communion with God through meditation, prayer and fasting. They yearn for their souls to rise heavenward and unite with God. Perhaps the best-known mystical statement on prayer is found in the *Zohar* regarding the wondrous dream of Jacob's ladder, whose base stood on the ground and whose top reached to the heavens. According to the *Zohar* this ladder is prayer.

Isaac Luria's branch of *kabbalah* asserts that people could attain union with the Divine Spirit through intense concentration. According to Luria, a person who performs a religious obligation is contributing to the meaning of the universe itself. Prayer plays an important part in the process of *tikkun* (mending) of the universe. Each *mitzvah* is to be accompanied by the recitation of a formula declaring that the act was done for the purpose of "uniting the Holy Blessed One, and His Shechinah, out of tears and love." Prayer is thus the vehicle by which a person's soul ascends to God.

According to kabbalists one can also influence the upper spheres of the universe, where God dwells, through prayer. The Zohar states: "Whoever prays with tears before the Almighty can procure the cancellation of any chastisement that has been decreed against him" (*I Zohar 223a*). To do this, one must be able to concentrate fully on the act of prayer. Thus, the true worshipper with proper *kavanah,* can change the spiritual world of the universe and bring themselves into an intimate relationship with God.

Kabbalists often noted the difficulty posed by petitionary prayer to God, who is unchanging. In their view, prayer cannot be offered to God as He is in Himself, but only to God as He is manifested in the ten divine spheres or luminaries through which God is revealed. Thus, for example, God cannot be directly entreated to show mercy. Rather, prayer must be directed to God as God is manifested in the divine sphere or attribute of lovingkindness.

Kabbalists substituted the concept of special intentions, known as *kavanot* for the older doctrine of *kavanah*. These so-called meditations on the realm of the divine spheres require mystics to concentrate on the actual realm of divine potencies and to direct their minds to the supernal mysteries that govern them, rather than to simply concentrate on the plain meaning of the various prayers.

In many mystical writings there is a connection between communion with God (*devekut*) and prophecy, which is the outcome of such union between human beings and God. Moses, the greatest of all the prophets, is described as a man who was able to achieve a lasting state of *devekut*. When this state of communion is realized, the Holy spirit encounters the mystic and gives him wondrous spiritual abilities.

WAYS TO GOD IN HASIDISM

As described previously, modern Hasidism as a religious and social movement springs from the teachings of the 18th century Rabbi Israel Baal Shem Tov. He taught that all people are equal before God – the ignorant as well as the learned – and that prayerful devotion and humility are more acceptable in heaven than intellectual attainments. He often sought communion with God in the woods and the fields, emphasizing that life itself is a divine manifestation.

One of the Baal Shem Tov's principal teachings was that every *mitzvah*, including daily worship, must be done with great enthusiasm. A mere mechanical and lifeless performance of prayers is of little value.

For the Hasid, prayer is frequently seen as one of the most important religious activities.

Hasidism incorporates a great deal of body movement into prayer. Vigorous swaying (known as *shuckling*), laughter, dancing, and singing *niggunim* (melodies without words) are ways that Hasidim seek to attain a state of ecstasy and self-forgetfulness during prayer.

KABBALAT SHABBAT

The opening worship service on Friday evening, preceding the *Maariv* evening service is called *Kabbalat Shabbat* (welcoming the Sabbath). It consists of six psalms (*Psalms 95–99; 29*) followed by the famous poem *Lecha Dodi*, composed in the sixteenth century by Rabbi Solomon Alkabets and then Psalms 92–93.

The *Kabbalat Shabbat* service was first introduced by the *kabbalists* of the sixteenth century, who flourished in Safed, Israel. The six psalms, symbolizing the six workdays of the week, were selected by Rabbi Moses Cordovero (1522–1570), who was the head of the school of mystics before Rabbi Isaac Luria in 1569. According to his kabbalistic view, the aim of morality is to secure the unification of all powers of the soul and place them under the control of divine wisdom. The numerical value of the initial letters of the six selected psalms *lamed, shin, yud, mem yud, nun* add up to 430 which equals the numerical value of *nefesh*, the Hebrew word for soul.

Psalm 29, the last of the initial six psalms, contains the name of God eighteen times, a corresponding to the eighteen times God is mentioned in the Shema section, recited at all morning and evening services. Eighteen is also reminiscent of the eighteen blessings of the *Amidah* prayer, and the eighteen times that the three patriarchs – Abraham, Isaac, and Jacob-- are mentioned together in the Hebrew Bible.

Rabbi Moses Cordovero was a brother-in-law of Rabbi Solomon Alkabets, whose poem *Lecha Dodi* is the outstanding feature of the *Kabbalat Shabbat* service.

YEDID NEFESH

The mystical poem *Yedid Nefesh* (Dearly Beloved), proclaiming the spirit of love between God and His people, was composed by Eliezer Askari, one of the kabbalistic disciples of Isaac Luria and Joseph Karo who lived in Safed in the sixteenth century. The poem is usually sung at the beginning of the Friday evening *Kabbalat Shabbat* service. *Yedid Nefesh* is an acrostic whose four stanzas contain the four-letter holy name of God. (*tetragrammaton*). The poet contemplates God as the cause of bliss and happiness, the single highest good of all human striving.

Soul mate, loving God, compassion's gentle source
Take my disposition and shape it to Your will.
Like a darting deer will I rush to You.
Before Your glorious presence humbly will I bow.
Let your sweet love delight me with its thrill
Because no other dainty will my hunger still.

How splendid is Your light, illumining the world.
My soul is weary yearning for Your love's delight.
Please, good God, do heal her; reveal to her Your face,
The pleasure of Your presence bathed in Your grace.
She will find strength and healing in Your sight.
Forever will she serve You, grateful with all her might.

What mercy stirs in You since days of old, my God.
Be kind to me, your own child; my love for You requite.
With deep and endless longing, I yearned for Your embrace,
To see my light in Your light, basking in Your grace.
My heart's desire finds me worthy in Your sight.
Do not delay Your mercy; please hide not Your light.

Reveal Yourself, Beloved, for all the world to see,
And shelter me in peace beneath Your canopy.
Illumine all creation, lighting up the earth,
And we shall celebrate You in choruses of mirth.

The time, my Love, is now; rush, be quick and bold.
Let Your favor grace me, in the spirit of days of old.

ANA BE'KOACH

Known by its opening phrase *Ana Be'koach* (with strength), this prayer precedes *Lecha Dodi*. It is ascribed to the mystical teacher Nechunya ben ha-Kanah who lived into the second half of the first century of the common era. However, this prayer was probably more likely composed in the circle of the thirteenth century Spanish kabbalists.

Originally part of a collection of kabbalistic prayers known as *Tefillat haYichud* (prayers of the unity of God), this hymn expresses the people of Israel's longing for deliverance from the Diaspora and implores God's support and protection. It consists of seven verses of six words each, whose initials form the 42-lettered Holy Name of God and similar mystical combinations. The initials of the second verse form the sentence *kera satan*, (silence Satan). The hymn is translated as follows:

We beg You.
With the strength of Your right hand's greatness, untie the
  bundled sins.
Accept the prayer of Your nation.
Strengthen us, purify us, Awesome One.
O Strong One, those who foster Your Oneness, guard them like
  the pupil of an eye.
Bless them, purify them, show them pity.
May Your righteousness always recompense them.
Powerful Holy One, with Your abundant goodness guide Your
  congregation.
One and only Exalted One, turn to Your nation which proclaims
  Your holiness.
Accept our entreaty and hear our cry, Knower of mysteries.
Praised be the Name of His glorious kingdom forever and
  forever.

LECHA DODI

The central feature of the *Kabbalat Shabbat* service is *Lecha Dodi*, a hymn known by the opening phrase of its refrain, Come my beloved friend. The initial letters of the first eight stanzas of the nine-stanza acrostic spell out the first and middle names of its author Solomon HaLevi (Alkabets), a Safed mystic of the early 16th century. The opening line and refrain translate: "Come my friend to meet the bride, let us welcome the presence of the Sabbath."

Inspired by talmudic accounts that described how the scholars of Safed used to honor and welcome the Sabbath, comparing it to a princess or bride, *Lecha Dodi* both reflects the practice of the Safed Kabbalists as well as the identification of the Sabbath with the *Shechinah*, the mystical archetype of Israel. Thus, the messianic motifs of the hymn echo talmudic concepts that associate redemption with the observance of the Sabbath.

Lecha Dodi employs vivid figures of speech to express the people of Israel's hope. Personifying the Sabbath as a bride, in the same sense that Israel is likened to a bride (in *Jeremiah 2:2*), the liturgical poem begins with the refrain "come my friend to meet the bride." This is based on a talmudic passage (*Shabbat 119a*) in which Rabbi Chanina and Rabbi Yannai are quoted as having used this expression to salute the Sabbath. Referring to Israel, the poet exclaims: "Come forth from your ruins. Long enough have you dwelt in the vale of tears. Shake off your dust and arise. Awaken, awake, utter a song. Why are your downcast? Why do you moan? Your God will rejoice over you as a bridegroom rejoices over his bride."

The title *Lecha Dodi* is borrowed from the *Song of Songs* (7:12), where an intense delight in rural life infuses the lines: "Come my beloved, let us go into the field, let us stay in the villages; let us go early to the vineyards..." Following their leader's example, Rabbi Isaac Luria's disciples were said to go outside the city limits of Safed into the open fields to welcome the Sabbath, singing the psalms and hymns which now comprise the Friday evening *Kabbalat Shabbat* service.

For kabbalists, the Sabbath, Knesset Israel, and the City of Jerusalem are all intertwined with the *sefirah* of *malchut,* which mystics call the *Shechinah.* According to kabbalah the Sabbath is a taste of the world to come. It is the archetype of the future world when the body and spirit are released to a higher level. Shabbat and redemption are two aspects of the same notion – restoration of reality to its primitive state of purity. For kabbalists, the inner core of *Lecha Dodi* expresses the concept of redemption of both the individual and the nation of Israel. The act of welcoming the Sabbath foretells a day when all will be Shabbat. (*i.e.*, a day of great redemption)

Lecha Dodi is translated as follows:

Come my beloved with chorus of praise
Welcome Shabbat the Bride, Queen of our days.

"Keep" and "remember" were uttered as one
By our Creator, beyond comparison.
Adonai is One and His name is One
Reflected in glory, in fame and in praise.
Come my beloved....

Come, let us greet Shabbat, Queen sublime,
Fountain of blessings in every clime.
Anointed and regal since earliest time,
In thought she preceded Creation's six days.
Come my beloved....

Holy, city, majestic, banish your fears.
Arise, emerge from your desolate years.
Too long have you dwelled in the valley of tears.
God will restore you with mercy and grace.
Come my beloved...

Arise and shake off the dust of the earth.
Wear glorious garments reflecting your worth.
Messiah will lead us all soon to rebirth.
Let my soul now sense redemption's warm rays.
Come my beloved...

Awake and arise to greet the new light,
For in your radiance the world will be bright.
Sing out, for darkness is hidden from sight.
Through you, Adonai His glory displays.
Come my beloved....

In your redemption you will never be shamed.
Be not downcast, you will not be defamed.
Sheltered by you will My poor be reclaimed.
The city renewed from its ruins is raised.
Come my beloved...

Then your destroyers will themselves be destroyed.
Ravagers, at great distance, will live in a void.
Your God then will celebrate you, overjoyed,
As a groom with his bride when her eyes meet his gaze.
Come my beloved....

Break out of your confines, to the left and the right.
Revere Adonai in whom we delight.
The Messiah is coming to gladden our sight,
Bringing joy and rejoicing in fullness of days.
Come my beloved...

Come in peace, soulmate, sweet Bride so adored,
Greeted with joy, in song and accord,
Amidst God's people, the faithful restored,
Come, Bride Shabbat; come, crown of days.

Come my beloved, with chorus of praise
Welcome Shabbat the Bride, Queen of our days.

ANIM ZEMIROT

Rabbi Yehuda Hechasid, son of Rabbi Samuel ben Kalonymus, the twelfth century scholar and mystic is the reputed author of the prayer *Anim Zemirot* (also known as *Shir HaKavod – Hymn of Glory*). *Anim*

Zemirot is generally recited responsively in traditional congregations at the close of the Sabbath morning service. The Ark is opened during its recitation in respect for the hymn's great holiness.

The poet weaves a tapestry of praises to God in the hymn, employing images from the Torah, the visions of the prophets, the Psalms, and the Song of Songs. He attempts to describe a God who is beyond all description, a God for whom he longs, but can never truly know.

Anim Zemirot is translated as follows:

Melodies I weave, songs I sweetly sing.
Yearning for Your presence, to You I long to cling.

Within Your sheltering hand my soul delights to dwell.
Grasping at Your mystery, captured by Your spell.

When speaking of Your glory, Your radiance sublime,
My heart cries out for Your love transcending time.

Thus, I sing Your glory in speech as well as song,
Declaring with my love: To You do I belong.

Never have I see You, yet I state Your praise,
Never having known You, I laud You and Your ways.

To Your assembled servants and in Your prophets' speech,
You hinted at Your glory, which lay beyond their reach.
The vastness of Your power, the marvel of Your might
Were mirrored in Your actions, reflected in their sight.

The faithful ones portrayed You, but never as You are.
They told of all Your deeds, imagined from afar.

They spoke of You with parables, in visionary thought,
While ever Your great oneness inhered in all they taught.

In vain did they describe You as one now young, now old,
With hair now dark, now gray – as if it could be told.

Youth and force in battle, old age on judgment day.
Like a seasoned soldier, whose hands will clear the way.

Adorned with triumph, a helmet on His head,
God's power and holiness instill His foes with dread.

God's head suffused with dew, bathed in radiant light,
And locks of hair covered with dewdrops of the night.

God takes pride in me with heavenly delight.
And God will be my crown, whose praise I will recite.

God's head do we envision as pure and beaten gold,
That bears His holy name in letters large and bold.

With dignity and kindness, with splendor that they share,
Yisrael, God's people, crown Him with their prayer.

Encircled in God's head with curly locks of youth,
Hair black as any raven, splendid as the truth.

Nothing is more precious among God's treasured sights,
Than Zion, seat of splendor, chief of God's delights.

God's exalted people adorn Him as a crown,
A royal diadem of beauty and renown.

God lifts and crowns the people He nurtured since their birth,
God loves and honors Israel far beyond their worth.

Through mutual devotion, expressed in song and rhyme,
I know that I approach God's presence so sublime.

Radiant and ruddy, His garments red as wine,
God crushes sinning nations like grapes pulled from a vine.

The knot of God's tefillin shone in humble Moses' eyes.
A vision of God's ways was his glimpse of paradise.

Raising up the humble, enthroned upon their praise,
God relishes His people, exalted through their ways.

Your word is based on truth from the start of all Creation.
Seek good for those who seek You in every generation.

Cherish all my songs as though Your very own.
May this, my joyous verse, approach Your holy throne.

My praise I humbly offer as a crown upon Your head.
For the incense we once gave, accept my prayer instead.

May the words of this my song be precious as the psalter,
Once offered You with sacrifice upon the Temples' altar.

My prayer seeks the Creator of the miracle of birth,
Master of beginnings whose justice fills the earth.

And when I chant my prayer, may You greet it with assent,
The scent of ancient offerings to You is my intent.

May You find sweet and pleasing my prayer and my song.
My soul goes out in yearning, for You alone I long.

BEREECH SHEMAI

There is a custom to read a portion of the *Zohar* (*Parashat Vayakhel*) that petitions God to reveal His redeeming power on the Sabbath during the Torah service. Some liturgical commentators have posited that this prayer may have been intended to indicate Judaism's rejection of the Christian doctrine that humanity is expected to believe that Jesus is "the son of God" in order to achieve salvation. The prayer also emphasizes the Jews' acceptance of Torah and the prophetic writings as expressing the truth, one of God's main attributes. The following is a translation of *Bareech Shemai* (Praised is Your Name)

Blessed be You, O Sovereign of the universe.
Praised be Your crown and Your dwelling place.
May Your favor rest upon Your people Israel for all eternity.
Reveal to Your people in Your sanctuary Your redeeming power
     of Your right hand.
Grant us the benign gift of Your light, and in mercy accept our
     supplications.
May it be Your will to prolong our life in well-being.

Let us be counted among the righteous, so that You may be merciful to us, and protect us and our dear ones and all Your people Israel.

You feed and sustain all.

You rule overall, over kings, for all dominion is Yours.

We are the servants of the Holy Blessed One, before whom and before whose glorious Torah we always bow.

Not in people do we put our trust, nor upon any angel do we rely, but upon the God of heaven, who is the God of truth, and whose Torah is truth, and whose prophets are prophets of truth, and who abounds in deeds of goodness and truth.

In God do we trust, and unto His holy and glorious name we utter praises.

May it be Your will to open our hearts to Your Torah, and to fulfill the wishes of our hearts and of the hearts of all Your people Israel, for good, life and peace.

THE KEDUSHAH: SANCTIFICATION PRAYER

The *Kedushah* is attached to the *Amidah* prayer in the morning and in the afternoon services. It is filled with mystical overtones, and contains a mosaic of biblical verses, many of which deal with angelic hosts singing God's praises. The introductory words of the *Kedushah* summon the congregation to join in the praise of God in the manner of angels, who keep calling to one another: "Holy holy holy is the Lord of Hosts, the whole world is filled with God's Presence. (*Isaiah 6:3*)

The congregational response, taken from the mystical prophet Ezekiel follows the verse "God's glory fills the universe." When one angelic chorus asks, "Where is God's glory?" another responds with praise: *Baruch kevod Adonai mimkomo* – Praised is God's glory throughout the universe. Mystics, as well as other contemporary worshippers, often imagine themselves in God's closest circle while reciting this prayer, joining with the ministering angels in chanting the most precious of praises.

In the opening chapter of the Book of Ezekiel, the prophet shares his mystical vision of God's throne, describing the angels as having one straight, unbent leg. As traditional Jews recite the *Kedushah* echoing the angels' praise of God, they too customarily stand erect in God's presence. There is also a custom of rising on one's toes during the repetitions of the word *kadosh* (holy), literally lifting one's praise toward the singing *seraphim* (fiery angels).

PRAYER FOR FALLING ASLEEP

According to the *Talmud*, one should repeat the first paragraph of the *Shema* before retiring to sleep. Some prayerbooks also include the mystical prayer about God's four archangels, Michael, Gabriel, Uriel, and Raphael.

First appearing in the book of Daniel, Michael was portrayed as the constant defender of the Jewish people in the *Pesikta Rabbati*, an early medieval compilation of legends. According to mystical tradition, Michael is a central figure on God's Divine Chariot. He is the guardian of the south side, portrayed as a lion in the Chariot. Michael is also assigned the role of grace in the *Merkavah*, angel of the right, representing the Divine sphere of *chesed* (grace). Frequently described as a high priest, Michael is also portrayed as bringing the souls of the righteous before God in the *Zohar*, an act which led to their inclusion in the kabbalistic world of emanation.

Raphael, from the Hebrew word *refuah*, is the angel of healing. In kabbalistic literature, Raphael has a high rank and is credited with a variety of missions. Among the four elements, he governs earth. In the colors of the rainbow, he represents green. According to other mystics, he commands the special host of angels known as *Ophanim*, which appear in the famous vision of God's Throne Chariot in chapter one of the *Book of Ezekiel*. In the Zohar itself, Raphael is the angel who dominates the morning hours, bringing relief to those who are ill.

Uriel means "God is my light." In the Zohar Uriel is identified as one of the four beasts (sometimes the lion, and at other times the eagle) that Ezekiel saw in the first chapter of his book. He is also identified as one of the four angels who shed light on the four winds of heaven. Uriel's light which is shed over the west is considered the most perfect form of light. The *Zohar (1 6b)* also ascribes a special function in connection with the sacrifices during first Temple times to Uriel. The altar (called *Ariel* in *Isaiah 29*), descended in the guise of a lion to crouch on the altar and swallow sacrifices was called Uriel. Uriel's appearance in the altar fire caused all those who saw the flames to change their ways and repent.

Mystics believe that calling on the four archangels in the following evening prayer is the way to plug into the infinite resource of God's energy.

In the name of the Lord, the God of Israel, may Michael be at my right hand; Gabriel at my left; before me, Uriel. Behind me, Raphael, and above my head the divine presence of God. (*To be said 3 times*)

KIDDUSH LEVANAH: BLESSING THE MOON

Because of its monthly reappearance, the moon is often considered an emblem of the people of Israel. Israel, like the new moon, has undergone phrases of persecution throughout its history, always emerging anew without being destroyed. Also like the moon, the Jewish people regularly reappear after being temporarily eclipsed. It is for this reason that a ceremony known as *kiddush levanah* was created centuries ago for sanctifying the new moon.

The new moon blessing is customarily recited in the open air when the moon is visible – between the fourth and the sixteenth of the month, preferably on a Saturday night after *Havdalah*, when traditional Jews are in a joyous frame of mind.

One of the passages of the blessing refers to the Creator by four synonyms whose first letters spell the name *Yaakov* (Jacob), thereby alluding to his descendants, the people of Israel. The passage reads "*Baruch yotzrecha . . . osecha. . . . konecha, borecha.*"

The expression "Long live David, King of Israel" in the blessing refers to *Psalm 89:38*, which predicts that David's dynasty shall "like the moon be established forever." The numerical value of this line in Hebrew "*David melech yisrael chai ve-kayam*" (819) is equal to that of *Rosh Chodesh* (the new month). Interestingly, this became the password of Bar Kochba's army.

The blessing of the new moon opens with a benediction praising the Creator of the celestial lights who ordained the monthly renewal of the moon. The Talmudic tractate *Sofrim* (20:1–2), prescribes several mystifying and mystical details in connection with the blessing:

- The blessing of the moon must take place at the end of the Sabbath when one is in a jovial mood and dressed in pleasant garments.
- The worshiper is expected to look directly at the moon, stand straight and erect with feet together, and recite the benediction.
- The worshiper should repeat *siman tov* – (a good sign) three times and perform three dancing gestures in the direction of the moon while saying "Just as I cannot touch you, may my enemies never be able to harm me" three times.
- Then the worshiper should say *shalom* – (peace) to his neighbor three times and go home with a happy heart.

The basic text of the new moon blessing is presented in the Talmudic tractates of *Sanhedrin 42a* and *Soferim 2:1*, and there have been many subsequent additions since that time. In the current Ashkenazi ritual, the blessing is usually introduced by the recitation of *Psalms 148:1–6* (in the Sephardic rite also *Psalm 8:4–5*) which is followed by the blessing praising God as the Sovereign over nature. Here is the text of the new moon blessing [Ashkenazic ritual]:

Rabbi Yochanan said: Whoever blesses the new moon at the proper time is considered as having welcomed the presence of the Shechinah.

Halleluyah. Praise God from the heavens. Praise God, angels on high.

Praise God, sun and moon and all shining stars. Praise God, highest heavens.

Let them praise the glory of God at whose command they were created, at whose command they endure forever and by whose laws nature abides. (*Psalm 148:1–6*).

When I behold Your heavens, the work of Your fingers, the
   moon,
and stars that You set into place.
What is man that You have been mindful of him,
mortal man that You have taken note of him.
Praised are You, *Adonai* our God, Sovereign of the Universe
whose word created the heavens, whose breath created all that
   they contain.
Statutes and seasons God set for them, that they should not
   deviate from their given task.
Gladly, they do the will of their Creator, whose work is
   dependable.
To the moon God spoke:
Renew yourself, crown of glory for those who were born in the
   womb, who also
are destined to be renewed and to extol their Creator for His
   glorious sovereignty.
Praised are You, God, who renews the months.
David, King of Israel, lives and endures. *Shalom Aleichem.*
May good fortune be ours, and blessing for the entire household
   of Israel.

PASSAGE FROM THE ZOHAR IN
HASIDIC PRAYERBOOKS

Many traditional Hasidic prayerbooks include recitation of the following passage from the *Zohar* on Friday night. In it the Sabbath is
personified and adorned with crowns given to her by God.

The mystery of Sabbath:
Sabbath is unification through oneness, which causes the
   mystery of oneness to dwell upon it.
Prayer, which the Sabbath raises up, unifies, and perfects the
   holy and precious throne through the mystery of oneness so
   that the divine and holy King may sit upon it.

When the Sabbath begins, she is made one and separates from
the other side (*i.e.*, evil) and all the forces of severity pass
away.
She remains unified with the holy light and is adorned with
many crowns by the holy King.
All the powers of ire and forces of severity are uprooted and
there is no evil dominion upon the worlds.
Her face is radiant with divine light and she is adorned below
with the holy people.

(*Zohar II: 135ab*)

PEREK SHIRA: CHAPTER OF SONG

Perek Shira: Chapter of Song is by far one of the most unique and
unusual volumes in all Jewish literature. According to some scholars,
the book is one of the oldest texts of *Merkavah* mysticism, the first
form of Jewish mysticism in the early centuries of the Common Era.
First mentioned in a polemical work of Salmon ben Jeroham, a tenth
century Jerusalemite, its liturgical use was revived in the mystical city
of Safed in the sixteenth century where it began to be recited as a prayer.

Perek Shira is a collection of sayings in praise of God and the
Creator. What makes the book mysterious and compelling is that the
sayings of praise have been placed in the mouth of God's creatures. All
creation, except humans, is represented – the natural and supernatural
orders, inanimate nature, the heavens and their hosts, the world of
plants, and the world of animals, each according to its kind. Together
the hymns comprise a kind of cosmic song of praise sung by the whole
of creation. Most of the hymns are biblical verses, the greater part of
them are citations from the *Book of Psalms*. The following are excerpts
from *Perek Shira*:

The heavens say: "The heavens declare the glory of God; the sky
proclaims God's handiwork. (*Psalm 19:1–2*)

The earth says: "The earth is God's and the fullness thereof, and
they that dwell in it" (*Psalm 24:1*), and also says: "From the end

of the earth we hear singing: glory to the righteous!" (*Isaiah 24:16*)

The Garden of Eden says: "Awake, O north wind, and come, you south; blow on my garden that the spices thereof may flow out." (*Song of Songs 4:6*)

Gehenna says: "For he has satisfied the longing soul and filled the hungry soul with goodness." (*Psalm 107:9*)

The desert says: "The arid desert shall be happy; the wilderness shall rejoice." (*Isaiah 35:1*)

The fields say: "God by wisdom founded the earth, but understanding God established the heavens." (*Proverbs 3:19*)

The waters say: "When he makes his voice heard, there is a rumbling of waters in the skies. He makes vapors rise from the ends of the earth." (*Jeremiah 51:16*)

The seas say: "God on high is mightier than the noise of many waters, than the mighty waves of the sea." (*Psalm 93:4*)

The rivers say: Let the rivers clap their hands, let the mountains together sing for joy." (*Psalm 98:8*)

The springs say: "And singers and dancers alike shall say: all my springs are in you." (*Psalm 87:7*)

The day says: "Day to day utters speech, and night to night expresses knowledge." (*Psalm 19:3*)

The night says: "To relate your steadfast love each morning and your faithfulness every night." (*Psalm 92:3*)

The sun says: "Sun and moon stand still on high as your arrows fly in brightness, your flashing spear in brilliance." (*Habbakuk 3:11*)

The moon says: "God appointed the moon for seasons, the sun knows his going down." (*Psalm 104:19*)

The stars say: "You alone are God, you have made heaven, the heaven of heavens, with all their host, the earth, and all things that are in it, the seas, and all that is therein, and you preserve them all, and the host of heavens worships you." (*Nehemiah 8:6*)

The clouds say: "God made darkness His secret place. His pavilion around about Him was dark water and thick clouds of the skies." (*Psalm 18:12*)

The clouds of glory say: "Also he burdens the thick cloud with an overflow, the cloud scatters lightning." (*Job 37:11*)

The winds say, "I will say to the north, 'Give back.' And to the south, 'Do not withhold.' Bring my sons from afar, and my daughters from the end of the earth." (*Isaiah 43:6*)

The lightning says: "God makes lightnings for the rain and brings the wind out of the treasuries." (*Psalm 135:87*)

The dew says "I will be to Israel like dew. He shall blossom like the lily and strike root like a tree of Lebanon." (*Hosea 14:6*)

The rains say "You, God, did send a bountiful rain, whereby You did strengthen Your inheritance when it languished." (*Psalm 68:10*)

The trees in the field say: "The trees of the forest shall sing for joy at the presence of God, for God comes to judge the earth." (*1 Chronicles 16:33*)

The vine says: Thus, says God. As when new wine is present in the cluster, one says: 'Do not destroy it, for there is good in it,' so will I do for the sake of My servants, and not destroy everything." (*Isaiah 65:8*)

The fig tree says: "He who guards the fig tree shall eat its fruit." (*Proverbs 27:18*)

The pomegranate says: "Your cheek is like a piece of pomegranate within its locks." (*Song of Songs 4:3*)

The palm tree says: "The righteous flourish like a palm tree, growing mighty like a cedar in Lebanon." (*Psalm 92:13*)

The stalk of wheat says: "A Song of Ascent. Out of the depths I have cried to you, O God." (*Psalm 130:1*)

The stalk of barley says: "A prayer of the afflicted, when he faints and pours out his complaint before God." (*Psalm 102:1*)

All the rest of the stalks say: "The meadows are clothed with flocks. The valleys are also covered over with corn. They shout for joy and sing." (*Psalm 65:14*)

The vegetables in the field say: "Watering her furrows abundantly, settling her ridges. You make it soft with showers and bless its growth." (*Psalm 65:11*)

The grasses say: 'May the glory of God endure forever. Let God rejoice in His works." (*Psalm 104:31*)

The rooster says: "At the time that the Holy Blessed One comes among the righteous ones who dwell in the Garden of Eden, all the trees of the Garden pour out fragrant spices and sing and offer praises. Then He too is aroused and offers praises." The rooster crows in seven voices:

The first voice says: "Lift up your heads, you gates and be lifted up you everlasting doors, that the King of glory shall enter. Who is this King of glory? The Lord strong and mighty, the Lord mighty in battle." (*Psalm 24:7*)

The second voice says: "Lift up your heads, you gates, and lift them up, you everlasting doors that the King of glory may enter. Who is the King of glory. The God of Hosts, He is the King of glory. Selah." (*Psalm 24:9*)

The third voice says: "Arise, you righteous ones, and busy yourselves with Torah so that your reward will double in the world to come." (*Ramban, Sha'ar HaGemul.*)

The fourth voice says: "I wait for your salvation, O God." (*Genesis 49:18*)

The fifth voice says: "How long will you sleep, lazy one?" (*Proverbs 6:9*)

The sixth voice says: "Do not love sleep lest you come to poverty. Open your eyes and you shall be satisfied with bread." (*Proverbs 20:13*)

The seventh voice says: "It is time to act for God. They have violated your Torah. (*Psalm 119:126*)

The chicken says: "He gives food to all flesh and His steadfast love endures for eternity." (*Psalm 136:25*)

The dove says: "I piped like a swift or a crane, I moaned like a dove. As my eyes all worn looked to heaven: 'My God, I am in straits. By my surety.'" (*Isaiah 38:14*)

The dove speaks before the Holy Blessed One, "Master of the Universe, may my food be as bitter as the olive but entrusted to your hand rather than sweet as honey and dependent on one of flesh and blood." (*Talmud Eruvin 186*)

The eagle says: "You, O God of Hosts, God of Israel, bestir yourself to bring nations to account. Have no pity on all of the treacherous villains." (*Psalm 59:6*)

The crane says: "Praise God with the lyre, with the ten stringed harp sing to Him." (*Psalm 33:2*)

The sparrow says: "Even the sparrow has found a home, and the swallow a nest for herself in which to set her young, near Your altar, O God of hosts, my king and my God." (*Psalm 84:4*)

The swallow says: 'That my whole being might sing hymns to you endlessly. O God, I will forever praise You." (*Psalm 30:13*)

The peacock says: "My help comes from God who made heaven and earth." (*Psalm 121:2*)

The desert bird says: "Light is sown for the righteous and happiness for the upright in heart." (*Psalm 97:11*)

The dove says: "Comfort, comfort my people, says your God." (*Isaiah 40:1*)

The stork says:" Speak tenderly to Jerusalem and declare to her that her term of service is over, that her sin is expiated. For she has received at the hand of God double for her sins." (*Isaiah 40:2*)

The raven says: "Who provides for the raven his provision when his young ones cry to God?" (*Job 38:41*)

The starling says: Their offspring shall be known among the nations, their descendants amid the peoples. All who see them shall recognize that they are a stock that God has blessed." (*Isaiah 61:9*)

The domestic goose says: "Praise God. Call on his name. Proclaim his deeds among the nations. Sing praises to him and speak of his wondrous acts." (*Psalm 105:1–2*)

The goose who lives in the desert, when he sees Israel engaged with Torah, says: "A voice rings out: 'Clear in the desert a road for God. Level in the wilderness a highway for our God.'" (*Isaiah 40:3*)

The chicken says: 'Trust in God forever, for God is an everlasting rock." (*Isaiah 26:4*)

The vulture says: "I will whistle to them and gather them, for I will redeem them. They shall increase and continue increasing." (*Zechariah 10:8*)

The butterfly says: "I will lift my eyes up to the mountains, from where does my help come?" (*Psalm 121:1*)

The locust says: "O Lord, you are my God. I will extol you. I will praise your name, for you have done marvelous things, counsels of steadfast faithfulness." (*Isaiah 25:1*)

The spider says: "Praise him with resounding cymbals, praise him with clanging cymbals." (*Psalm 150:5*)

The fly, when Israel is not engaged with Torah, says: "A voice rings out: 'Proclaim.' Another asks: 'What shall I proclaim?' All flesh is grass, and all its goodness is like the flowers of the field.'" (*Isaiah 40:6*)

The sea monsters say: "Praise God, you who are on earth, all sea monsters and ocean depths." (*Psalm 148:7*)

Leviathan says: "Praise God for he is good, his steadfast love is eternal." (*Psalm 136:1*)

The fish say: "The voice of God is on the waters, the God of glory thunders, God is upon the mighty waters." (*Psalm 29:3*)

The frog says: "Blessed be the name of his glorious majesty forever and ever. "*Psalm 72:19*).

The small cow who is ritually pure says: "Who is like you, O God, among the gods? Who is like you, glorious in holiness, fearful in praises, doing wonders?" (*Exodus 15:11*)

The large cow who is ritually pure says, "Sing joyously to God, our strength. Raise a shout to the God of Jacob." (*Psalm 81:2*)

The small cow who is ritually impure says: "Do good, O God, to those who are good, to the upright in heart." (*Psalm 125:4*)

The large cow who is ritually impure says: "You shall enjoy the fruit of your labors. You shall be happy and prosper." (*Psalm 128:2*)

The camel says: "God roars from on high, He makes His voice heard from its holy dwelling. He roars aloud over his earthly abode." (*Jeremiah 25:30*)

The horse says: "As the eyes of slaves follows their master's hands, as the eyes of a slave girl follow the hand of her mistress, so our eyes are toward God, awaiting his favor." (*Psalm 123:2*)

The mule says: "All the kings of the earth shall praise you, O God, for they have heard the words you spoke." (*Psalm 138:4*)

The donkey says: "Yours, O God, is the greatness and power and glory and victory and majesty. All that is in heaven and on earth belongs to You. O God, Yours is the kingdom and You are exalted as head above all." (*1 Chronicles 29:11*)

The bull says: "Then Moses and the children of Israel sang this song to God. They said: 'I will sing to God for He has triumphed, horse and driver He has thrown into the sea.'" (*Exodus 15:1*)

The animals of the field say: "Blessed be the One who is good and does good."(*Psalm 119:68*)

The deer says: "And I will sing of Your strength, extol every morning Your faithfulness, for You have been my haven, a refuge in time of trouble." (*Psalm 59:17*)

The elephant says: "How great are your works O God, how very deep are your thoughts." (*Psalm 92:6*)

The lion says: "God goes forth like a warrior, like a fighter He whips up his rage. He yells, he roars aloud, he charges upon his enemies." (*Isaiah 42:13*)

The bear says: "Let the desert and its towns cry aloud, the villages where Kedar dwells. Let Sela's inhabitants shout, call out from the peaks of the mountains. Let them do honor to God and tell His glory in the coastlands." (*Isaiah 42:11–12*)

The wolf says: "In all charges of misappropriation – pertaining to an ox, an ass, a sheep, a garment, or any other loss, whereof one party alleges. 'This is it' – the case of both parties shall come before God. He whom God declares guilty shall pay double to the other." (*Exodus 22:8*)

The fox says: "Woe to him who builds his house by unrighteousness and his chambers by injustice. That uses his neighbor's service without pay and does not give him his wages." (*Jeremiah 22:13*)

The cat says: "I pursued my enemies and overtook them. I did not turn back till I destroyed them." (*Psalm 18:38*)

The insects say: "Let Israel rejoice in its maker, let the children of Zion exult in their king." (*Psalm 149:2*)

The serpent says: "God supports all who fall and makes all who are bent down stand upright." (*Psalm 145:14*)

The scorpion says: "God is good to all, and God's mercy is upon all His works." (*Psalm 145:9*)

The snail says: "Like a snail that melts away as it moves, like a woman's stillbirth, may they never see the sun." (*Psalm 58:9*)

The ant says: "Go to the ant, you sluggard, consider her ways and be wise." (*Proverbs 6:6*)

The mouse says: "And you are righteous about all that befalls us, for you act in truth and we have done evil." (*Nehemiah 9:33*)

The rat says: "Let everything that has breath praise God, Halleluyah." (*Psalm 150:6*)

The dogs say: ""Come, let us bow down and kneel, bend the knee before God our Maker." (*Psalm 95:6*)

Blessed be the Lord, God, God of Israel, who alone does wonders. And blessed be His glorious name for ever. May His glory fill the entire earth. Amen and Amen.

TIKKUN CHATZOT: MIDNIGHT SERVICE

Midnight prayers, instituted by the Safed kabbalists of the 16th century, are known as *Tikkun Chatzot*. They were designed to maintain the memory of the Temple that was destroyed, which resulted in the exile of the Divine glory. The Safed mystics prescribed the reading of Psalms 137, 79, 42, 43, 111, 51, 126 for *Tikkun Chatzot*, as well as petitions and lamentations connected with the loss of Jewish independence. The observance of *Tikkun Chatzot* prevailed among the extremely pious mystically minded Jews who adhered to the teachings of Isaac Luria. Luria's own *siddur*, known as *Nusach Ari* abounds in meditations, based upon the premise that no prayer should be recited without concentrating one's mind. Most of these meditations (*kavanot and yichudim*) direct the worshiper's mind to the mystical significance of the religious act that he is about to perform.

SABBATH CUSTOMS AND THEIR ZOHARIC INTERPRETATIONS

The *Zohar* III: 272b explains that the head of the household must accomplish ten things at the Sabbath table, corresponding to the ten *sefirot*. Although many of these customs are rabbinic practices, the enumeration of ten central customs and the associated symbolism are Zoharic:

1. Light at least two Sabbath candles. The woman head of the household lights at least two Sabbath candles at the table before the onset of the Sabbath, corresponding to the two versions of the Sabbath law in the Decalogue. In the *Zohar*, the candles symbolize *Hesed* (mercy), and the table symbolizes *Din.* (severity). Symbolically, this act dispels *Din* from the table.

2. Bless the cup of wine: Traditionally, the male head of the household recites the *Kiddush*, the Sabbath blessing over wine at the table. The first part of the *Kiddush*, taken from the biblical description of the first Sabbath, is associated with *Yesod*, a masculine *sefirah*. The second section is associated with the feminine *Malchut*. Together,

the kiddush symbolizes the unification of masculine and feminine *sefirot*.

3. Perform the ritual handwashing before breaking bread: This rabbinic law is a requirement before eating bread. The *Zohar* requires that one hold a cup filled with water in the right hand, which symbolizes *Hesed*, pass the cup to the left hand, which symbolizes *Din*, and pour it first upon the right hand then pass the cup again and pour upon the left. This is done so that the priority of *Hesed* over *Din* on the Sabbath is emphasized.

4. Put two loaves of bread on the table: Two loaves are traditionally used to recall the double portion of manna that rained down on the Sabbath. According to the *Zohar* the two loaves placed together symbolize the union of *Malchut* and *Tiferet*. The *Zohar* requires that the diners eat from the lower of the two loaves, when one is placed on top of the other, to symbolize the lower *sefirot*, especially *Malchut*.

5. Eat three festive meals. The major meals of the Sabbath are Friday evening, Saturday lunch, and later Saturday following the late afternoon service. According to the *Zohar*, these meals ceremoniously invoke the power of *Malchut, Keter* and *Tiferet*, respectively. Special songs (*zemirot*) are sung at each of the meals, many of which were composed as hymns to the *sefirah* associated with that meal.

6. Discuss Torah at the table: According to the rabbinic tradition, the *Shechinah* dwells at any table where Torah is discussed.

7. Welcome poor guests at the table. Charitable concern for the poor is a feature of the social consciousness of the *Zohar*. The poor are believed to bring special merit to the table and aid in the achievement of unity.

8. Perform ritual handwashing after the meal: This is a rabbinic custom called "final water" (*mayyim aharonim*). It is done after the meal before reciting the blessing after food. The *Zohar* explains that this custom is performed to cleanse the hands of evil and to remove the impurities that cling to them. It is also intended to wash away particles of food which are then considered a concession and nourishment to the evil forces.

9. Recite the blessing after food: According to the Zohar this rabbinic practice is associated with the *sefirah Hesed.* The *Zohar* explains that one who says this blessing with intention will invoke *Hesed* upon the world.
10. Bless a final cup of wine: According to rabbinic tradition a final cup of wine is blessed following the blessing after the food.

Other mystical customs include the circling the Sabbath table: Some do this twice at the Sabbath meal, once to the right and once to the left. Walking around the table sets it off as holy space and shows one's awareness of its sanctity. There is another custom called "holy silence." At some Sabbath tables there is silence without any conversation whatsoever, to encourage *devekut (clinging one's soul to God during the meal).*

These practices illustrate the way Jewish mystics reinterpret traditional practices in light of mystical teachings.

EYSHET CHAYIL: WOMAN OF VALOR

The mystics also introduced completely new customs. One such innovation introduced by the Safed Kabbalists is the custom of singing Woman of Valor (*Eyshet Chayil*) as a hymn at the Sabbath table. The selections from the *Book of Proverbs* praise the homemaker and allude to the *Shechinah.* In kabbalistic thought, the woman of valor is a hymn of praise for the homemaker and for the *sefirah* of *malchut.* After the recitation of the Woman of Valor some have the mystical custom of preparing themselves for the Sabbath meal by reciting:

"Prepare the meal of perfect faith, which is the delight of the
    Holy King.
Prepare the meal of the King."

Before the Friday night Sabbath meal some add:

"This is the meal of the *Chakal Tappuchin* and *Ze'ir Anpin* and the
Holy Ancient One come to join her in the meal."

The holy *Chakal Tappuchin* ("field of holy apples) is the term that the *Zohar* uses for the *Shechinah*, the *sefirah* of *Malchut*, which is manifested on the Sabbath eve. The *Zohar* also considers the Sabbath to be the most propitious occasion for unitive and restorative mysticism through human sexual intercourse. Sexual intercourse on the Sabbath eve produces the special Sabbath soul. Therefore, the Sabbath is the time when a righteous couple should have sexual contact.

ZEMIROT: TABLE SONGS

The *zemirot* sung during the Sabbath meals and at the close of the Sabbath sum up the very essence of holy joyousness that has been the keynote of Judaism. These songs and hymns, composed at a very early date, became particularly popular during the sixteenth century through kabbalistic influence. The custom of singing table songs, adding light and joy to the Jewish soul, is said to be two thousand years old. The ancient philosopher Philo, describing the life led by the ascetic Essenes, mentions their custom of singing table hymns in appreciation of God's continuous vigilance and goodness.

The tunes of the *zemirot*, reflecting the experiences of Israel, are mostly adapted from local folk tunes that eventually became characteristically Jewish. The texts of two kabbalistic *zemirot* follow.

Yah Ribbon Olam

Yah Ribbon Olam (Eternal Master of Worlds) is a hymn written in Aramaic by Rabbi Israel Najara, one of the most prolific Hebrew writers of the sixteenth century. His *Zemirot Yisrael*, comprised of 346 poems, was published at the end of the sixteenth century, and it soon became the most popular songbook among the Jewish communities in the orient. Israel Najara was one of the prominent members of the kabbalistic school at Safed in the Upper Galilee. The initial letters of the verses of *Yah Ribbon Olam* form the name "Yisrael", by which the poet's memory is immortalized.

Though *Yah Ribbon Olam* contains no allusion to the Sabbath, it is chanted on Friday evenings in all parts of the world. After describing the wonders of God's creation, the kabbalistically inspired poet, concludes with a prayer for the redemption of Israel and the restoration of Jerusalem, "the city of beauty."

Here is the text of the song in transliterated Hebrew and in translation:

Yah ribon alam v'almaya,
Ant hu malka melech malchaya
Ovad gevurteich v'timhaya
Sh'far kodamach l'hachavaya

Sh'vachin asader tzafra v'ramsha
Lach eleah kadisha divra chol nafsha
Irin kadishin uvnei enasha
Cheivat bara v'ofei shemaya

Ravr'vin ovdach v'takifin
Macheich ramaya v'zakeif k'fifin
Lu y'chei g'var sh'nin alfin
La yei-ol g'vurteich b'chuchb'naya

Elaha di lei y'kar urvuta
P'rok yat anach mipum aryavata
V'apeik yat amach migo galuta
Amach di v'chart mikol umaya

L'mikd'shach tuv ul-kodesh kudshin
Ata di vei yechednun ruchin v'nafshin
Vizamrun lach shirin v'rachashin
Birush leim karta d'shufraya

Almighty Master of worlds, of everything
You are the King who rules every king,
Your wonders and deeds leave us marveling,
It would be good to sing Your glory.

Morning and evening I will sing of Your worth
For with You, holy God, we all had birth,

Spirits in heaven and people on earth
Beasts in the field and birds on the wing.

Your deeds are mighty for strong and weak
You humble the proud and honor the meek
If a thousand years I could live and speak
I could not reveal all the wonders You bring

Dear God, to whom all glory goes,
O save Your flock from lion-like foes,
Set free Your people from exile's woes,
Of all nations You chose us, to You we cling

Return to Your Temple, Your holiest place,
Where spirits and souls will rejoice in Your grace
And sing to Your glory with shining face,
In Your city, Jerusalem, as lovely as spring.

Yom Zeh Le'Yisrael

The table hymn *Yom Zeh Le'Yisrael* ("This Day is for Israel") was composed by the mystic Isaac Luria. Its first stanza sets the mood for the hymn – a mixture of spiritual and physical pleasure, a divine commandment coupled with bodily enjoyment. Here are excerpts from the first and last stanzas of the hymn:

This day is for Israel light and rejoicing
A Sabbath of rest
You bade us, standing assembled at Sinai,
That all the years through which we should keep your behest
To set a table full-laden, to honor the Sabbath of rest…

Restore us our shrine – remember our ruin
Save now and comfort the sorely oppressed
Now sitting at Sabbath, all singing and praising
The Sabbath of rest.

MELAVE MALKAH

The departing Sabbath Queen is honored with special festivity hymns and songs at the conclusion of the Sabbath, bidding farewell to the holiness of the day and ushering in the new week with a plea for deliverance, health, and sustenance. The meal eaten on this occasion is known as *seudat melaveh malkah*, meaning that the outgoing queen is being *accompanied* by those who honor and cherish her. Some have the custom of preceding the melaveh *malkah* meal with the words: "Prepare the meal of perfect faith, this is the meal of David, the Messiah King." The Prophet Elijah figures prominently in the hymns of Saturday night, for according to popular tradition, he is to appear as the forerunner of the Messiah at the beginning of the new week.

Under kabbalistic influence, today's Hasidim customarily delay the conclusion of the Sabbath as much as possible by prolonging the *melaveh malkah* observance with songs and hymns.

Kabbalistic Customs Associated with Prayer Garments

THE *TALLIT*

The *tallit* or prayer shawl is the prayer garment that connotes religious responsibility. Its fringes (*tzitzit*) remind worshippers to perform *mitzvot*(commandments). Traditionally, males (as well as by females in more liberal settings) wear the *tallit* during morning services. The kabbalistic custom for donning the *tallit* begins by holding the *tallit* above one's head with both hands while reciting the blessing, and then draping it over the head. Then, grasping the four corners of the *tallit* in one hand (some only grasp the two corners on the right side of the *tallit*), one places the fringes over the left shoulder and recites *Psalm 36:8–11*:

> Bestow Your faithful care on those devoted to You
> And Your beneficence on upright men.
> Let not the foot of the arrogant tread on me,
> Or the hand of the wicked drive me away.
> There lie the evildoers, fallen,
> Thrust down, unable to rise.

These verses express the feeling that being wrapped in a *tallit* is like being enfolded in God's wings, as well as delight in the sense of closeness created by wearing the garment which corresponds to God's raiment of light and from which God's lovingkindness flows.

TEFILLIN

Tefillin (also known as phylacteries) are small leather boxes that contain parchment scrolls inscribed with various Biblical passages, including the *Shema* prayer. They are worn at morning services (except for the Sabbath and festivals) by men (and also by women in more liberal settings). One box, attached to a leather headband, is worn on the head (*tefillin shel rosh*), and a second box is worn on the bicep, attached by a leather strap that is wound around the non-dominant arm and hand in a designated pattern. The Biblical passages on the scrolls in the *tefillin* stress the duty of loving and serving God with one's whole being.

Kabbalists have a custom of reciting a prayer imbued with mystical significance after donning the *tefillin shel rosh* (the head tefillin):

> You give it openhandedly, feeding every creature to its heart's content. (*Psalm 145:16*)

This verse alludes to the four compartments of the head *tefillin* and to various aspects of the arm t*efillin* which have mystical meaning. The crown of the *tefillin* acts as a corporeal symbolic pattern, representing the supernal reality of the upper worlds of the kabbalah. The *Zohar* offers this interpretation:

> Whenever one places *tefillin* on the head and arm, a voice goes forth every day to all the creatures of the Holy Chariot and to all the angels in charge of our prayers: "Give honor to the image of the King. (*Tikkun Zohar, no. 47*)

This mutual relationship is further described in the prayer *Shir HaKavod*:

> His splendor is upon me and my splendor is upon Him.

The Kabbalah and Jewish Festivals

Proponents of Jewish mysticism view the Jewish festivals as unitive and restorative sacraments. The special rituals of each holidays serve various functions in Jewish mysticism, including realigning and reuniting the configuration of the *sefirot*. The following section summarizes the connections between Jewish mysticism and festival rituals.

ROSH HASHANAH: JEWISH NEW YEAR

Rosh Hashanah is the beginning of the Jewish new year. It is an opportunity to begin anew and petition God to be sealed in the Book of Life. Jewish mystics believe that the aspect of divine judgment is aroused on Rosh Hashanah through the ascendancy of the *sefirah Din*. "On Rosh Hashanah the power of severity is awakened above. Therefore, every person must arouse himself below to complete repentance. For by this, merciful love is awakened" (*Yesh Sakhar 22a*).

The rituals of Rosh Hashanah mitigate the power of the *sefirah* of *Din* by empowering the *sefirah* of *Hesed* (Mercy). Repentance helps to keep the *sefirah* of *Din* in check.

The *shofar* (ram's horn) also symbolizes the predominance of *Hesed* over *Din*. The *shofar* is sounded more than one hundred times on Rosh Hashanah, activating and creating a configuration of the *sefirot* in which the *sefirah* of *Hesed* predominates. In kabbalistic thinking, the *shofar* itself symbolizes *Binah* (intuitive understanding) and emphasizes *Hesed* since it is the *sefirah* that precedes *Hesed*.

The Torah reading for the first day of Rosh Hashanah details Isaac's assumption of the right of primogeniture over his brother Ishmael, symbolizing the supremacy of *Din* on that day.

The story of the birth of Isaac and his father Abraham's attempt to sacrifice him is read on the second day of Rosh Hashanah as part of the Torah service. In Jewish mysticism, Abraham is linked with the *sefirah* of *Hesed* because of the biblical verse: "Deal graciously (*hesed*) with my master Abraham" (*Genesis 24:12*). Isaac is associated with *Din* (severity and judgment) through the biblical phrase "the fear (*pachad*) of Isaac (*Genesis 31:42*).

YOM KIPPUR: THE DAY OF ATONEMENT

Yom Kippur is a time for afflicting one's soul. In kabbalistic thought, Yom Kippur is the next stage in the process of reuniting the *sefirah* of *Tiferet* and *Malchut* which began on Rosh Hashanah through the softening power of *Din*. On Yom Kippur, the *sefirah Binah*, the source of *Hesed*, prevails and uplifts the *Shechinah* in preparation for reunion with *Tiferet*.

For the mystic, the *Kol Nidrei* prayer which is chanted on Yom Kippur eve is, an invocation to the highest *sefirot* to release *Tiferet* and *Malchut* from the bonds of *Din* to facilitate their union. The drama of reunification continues throughout the month of *Tishri*.

SUKKOT: THE FESTIVAL OF BOOTHS

The festival of *Sukkot* follows the holy day of Yom Kippur. It is observed by dwelling in small booths and waving the four species (palm branch, willows, etrog and myrtle) both in the home and in the synagogue.

For kabbalists, the construction of the sukkah is symbolically linked with the seven *sefirot* from *Hesed* to *Malchut*, each of which corresponds to one of the seven days of the holiday. The booth itself symbolizes *Binah*, the divine mother, who protects the seven lower *sefirot*.

The Zohar introduced a Sukkot ritual that has gained widespread acceptance in Jewish circles today. Because of the association between the seven lower *sefirot* and the seven days of Sukkot, the Zohar created a ritual that symbolically invites the *sefirah* linked with that day as a guest to the sukkah. Since biblical personalities were identified with each *sefirah*, the custom of welcoming mystical guests (*ushpizin*) into the sukkah emerged. This custom of inviting seven biblical guests (Abraham, Isaac, Jacob, Joseph, Moses, Aaron, and David) rests on a kabbalistic statement that the *Shechinah* shelters the sukkah beneath its wings, and Abraham, in the company of six righteous men, enter to partake of the hospitality of Jewish people who properly observe the precept of the sukkah. Abraham is symbolized by the *sefirha* of *Hesed*, Isaac by the *sefirah* of *Din*, Jacob by the *sefirah* of *Tiferet*, Moses by the *sefirah* of *Netzach*, Aaron by the *sefirah* of *Hod*, Joseph by the *sefirah* of *Yesod*, and David by the *sefirah* of *Malchut*. Special greetings are recited for each guest, and wall decorations of these greetings and biblical personalities often adorn the sukkah walls. The following is the ritual greeting recited during the *ushpizin* ritual of the first day.

> Be seated, be seated, exalted guests. Be seated, be seated, holy guests.
> Be seated, be seated, guests of faithfulness.
> Be seated in the shade of the Holy Blessed One.
> Worthy is our portion, worthy is the portion of Israel,
> as it is written: For God's portion is His people, worthy is the portion of Israel,
> as it is written: For God's portion is His people, Jacob the lot of His heritage.
> For the sake of the unification of the Holy Blessed One and His Presence,
> to unify the Name "*Yod Hei*" with "*Vov Hei*"
> in perfect unity through Him who is hidden and inscrutable.
> I pray in the name of all Israel
> May it please you, Abraham, my exalted guest,
> That all the other exalted guests dwell here with me and with you –
> Isaac, Jacob, Joseph, Moses, Aaron, and David.

The *lulav* (palm branch) and *etrog* (citron) are also symbolically associated with the *sefirot*. The seven components of the *lulav* and *etrog* are also symbolic of the seven lower *sefirot*. The tall palm branch (*lulav*) is associated with the masculine *sefirah Yesod*. The round citron (*etrog*), with feminine connotations, symbolizes *Malchut*. The three myrtle branches (*hadassim*) suggest *Hesed, Din* and *Tiferet*, and the two willow branches (*aravot*) denote *Netzach* and *Hod*. The palm branch is waved during Sukkot services in six directions (east, south, west, north, up, and down), each direction corresponding to another *sefirah*, thus symbolizing the unity of the lower six *sefirot*.

Finally, on the last day, called Simchat Torah, the Torah reading begins anew with the story of creation. For the Jewish mystic, this holiday completes the unification of *Tiferet* and *Malchut* that began on Rosh Hashanah.

THIRTEEN ATTRIBUTES

The mystics followed the custom of repeating the Thirteen Divine attributes of God aloud during the service for taking out the Torah scroll on the weekdays of the festivals of Sukkot, Passover, and Shavuot. It is now customary to repeat these attributes aloud three times at each recitation.

These Godly attributes first appear in the *Torah* (*Exodus 34:6–7*). They are not meant to describe the essence of God philosophically, but rather to represent God as the source and fountain of all ethical behavior. These attributes are intended to serve as the standard for human morality:

> The Lord, the Lord is a merciful and gracious God,
> Slow to anger and abounding in kindness and truth.
> He extends kindness to the thousandth generation,
> Forgives iniquity, transgression and sin and clears the
>   guiltless.

PASSOVER: FESTIVAL OF FREEDOM

The festival of Passover celebrates the Israelites' exodus from Egypt and their liberation after four hundred years of slavery. For Jewish mystics, Passover symbolizes a victory over the demonic forces that prevail in the world as a result of the separation of *Malchut* and *Tiferet*. The absence of unity in the divine realm produces an abundance of *Din* and converts the *sefirah Malchut* to a source of suffering that is radiated upon the world. Only the reunification of the *Shechinah* with *Tiferet* can correct this situation. Egyptian slavery and the eventual deliverance are both the result of and symbolic of this process.

According to rabbinic legend, wherever Jews go into exile the *Shechinah* accompanies them for protection. According to another interpretation, exile is a punishment for the religious failures of the Israelites, and the *Shechinah* goes into exile along with the Israelites. For Jewish mystics, the liberation from Egypt symbolizes the redemption of the *Shechinah* from Her own exile and the beginning of her restoration to unity with *Tiferet*.

The many Passover rituals all have kabbalistic symbolism. In Jewish mysticism, *matzah* (unleavened bread) refers to the *Shechinah* in exile, which is impoverished due to her separation from *Tiferet*.

Leavened bread (*hametz*) symbolizes evil powers. For mystics, leaven is an allegory for the power of demonic forces over good.

The *seder* ritual is intended to reunite the *Shechinah* with *Tiferet*. Participants around the table customarily lean to the left. For kabbalists, this symbolizes *Binah*, which appears on the left in the diagram of the *sefirot*, and which is the *sefirah* of freedom. The three pieces of matzah on the *seder* table symbolize the *sefirot* of *Tiferet*, *Malchut* and *Yesod*. The middle matzah, symbolizing *Malchut*, is broken in half to suggest that *Malchut* is divided between the two male *sefirot*, *Tiferet* and *Yesod*, until she is finally reunited with her mate *Tiferet*. The hidden matzah, used for the *afikoman*, is linked with *Binah*, the hidden source of freedom.

The four cups of wine imbibed during the seder are associated with the four *sefirot* of *Chochmah*, *Binah*, *Tiferet* and *Malchut*, and symbolize the stages in the process of uniting *Tiferet* and *Malchut*. The bitter herbs (*maror*) suggest the bitterness that plagues *Tiferet* while it is separate from *Malchut*. The *haroset* (a mixture of apples, nuts, and wine) symbolizes the sweetness of redemption. The *seder* culminates in the temporary reunion of *Tiferet* and *Malchut* and the liberation from the dominion of evil.

SHAVUOT

Shavuot is the third and last of the pilgrimage festivals, commemorating the Israelites receiving the Torah on Mount Sinai. Jewish mystics understood this festival to be the culmination of the unification of *Tiferet* and *Malchut*. Unlike the pilgrimage festivals of Passover and Sukkot, Shavuot is celebrated for only one day in the Bible. Jewish mystics explain that this is because on Shavuot there is complete unity whereas on the other festivals there is only anticipation of unity.

Because Shavuot is the prototype of unity, Jewish mystics invented special rituals for its celebration. The *Zohar* introduced the practice of the *Tikkun Leil Shavuot*, the custom of staying awake all night on the eve and engaging in devotional preparation for the anniversary of receiving the *Torah* on Mount Sinai. In mystical symbolism, the Written *Torah* is associated with *Tiferet* and the Oral *Torah* is linked with *Malchut*. The *tikkun* ritual is designed to hasten the divine marriage by joining *Tiferet* and *Malchut*.

The ritual of *Tikkun Leil Shavuot* is conducted from midnight to dawn, when the *Malchut* dominates. The marriage ceremony between *Tiferet* and *Malchut* is considered complete when the Written *Torah* is read during the Shavuot morning service.

AKDAMUT

The *Akdamut* prayer is traditionally chanted on the first day of Shavuot before the reading of the *Torah*. This mystical hymn was composed in Aramaic by Rabbi Meir ben Isaac of the eleventh century. It consists of 99 verses arranged alphabetically. The acrostically arranged hymn is comprised of a twofold alphabet, the name of the author and that of his father, and the short petition: "*Meir Baer rebbe Yitzchak* and *yigdal batorah uv'maa'sim tovim amen, vechazak ve'amatz*". There are ten syllables to each verse, and one rhyme which runs throughout the entire poem. This hymn deals with the indescribable greatness of God, the excellence of the Torah and the future hope of Israel.

Consisting of two parts, the *Akdamut* serves as an introduction to the reading of the Ten Commandments from the Torah. The first part describes the unspeakable majesty of God who created heaven and earth. The second part presents a dialogue between persecuted Israel and those who try to persuade him to change his faith. which he clings to affectionately and tenaciously. A glowing description of the hoped-for messianic era then follows, mentioning the contest between the legendary monsters, *Leviathan* and *Behemot*. The battle ends with the destruction of both. In kabbalistic literature the *Leviathan* is identified with evil, which is destined to disappear in messianic times.

A translation of the *Akdamut* prayer that is typically recited during the Festival of Shavuot follows:

> Before reading the ten divine commands, O let me speak in awe two words, or three,
> Of the One who wrought the world and sustained it since time's beginning.
> At God's command is infinite power, which words cannot define.
> Were all the skies parchment and all the reeds pens, and all the oceans ink,
> And all who dwell on earth scribes, God's grandeur could not be told.
>
> Sovereign over the heavens above, God reigns supreme on earth below.
> God launched creation unaided and contains it in the bounds of His law.
>
> Without weariness God created, only by divine will, uttered in a gentle sound.

God wrought His works in six days, then established His
    glorious sovereignty
over the life of the universe.
Myriads of angelic hosts serve God, divine messengers that
    propel life's destiny
They arise each morning to their calling. All the celestial beings
    join in a chorus of praise.
In unison they call to one another: All the earth is full of the
    glory of the thrice Holy One.
In a mighty roar, as the thundering noise of vast water, moving
    amidst the heavenly spheres
Where the divine light glows brilliant the angelic hosts proclaim
    their words of adoration:
Praised be God's glory
By every whispering lip from the place of His abode which is
    everywhere.
All the celestial hosts roar their response in awe:
The splendor of God's dominion is acclaimed from age to age.
Yet dearer to God than this is the song of the children of
    Israel,
Rising to Him morning and evening, in free outpourings of
    adoration.
Chosen to be the faithful servants of His will, they continually
    rehearse God's praises,
Who summoned them in love to pursue the labors of Torah,
And accepts their supplications and entreaties, which weave a
    crown of glory for the Almighty.

The Eternal cherishes their prayers and keeps them ever before
    Him,
Thus, declaring the greatness of Israel who reiterate that God is
    One.
Israel acclaims the glory of the Ruler of the universe and offers
    God homage before kings and princes.
They all gather and ask in wonder,

Who is this your beloved, O fair one, for whom you brave the
    perils of the lion's den?
If you but join our fold, we would cover you with splendor and
    glory.
In every land would we ratify your every wish.

A wise reply is Israel's: How can you know God with your
    foolish minds?
How compare the glories you bestow with the glory that is
    God's,
With the splendor of His deeds in the hour of our deliverance,
When the light divine will shine on us, while darkness covers
    your mocking multitudes,
When God will manifest His glorious might and render His foes
    their due,
And triumph to the people abounding in virtue whom God has
    loved.

Joy unmarred will reign in hearts ennobled, pure, Jerusalem will
    rise again.
Her exiled children will come back to her.
Day and night God will shed His glory on her and build in her
    anew His sacred shrine of praise.

The righteous will possess the reward for their service.
They will dwell before their Creator, arrayed on golden
    thrones,
With seven steps ascending, resplendent as the azure of the sky
    and the brightness of the stars.

They will acclaim God:
It is God we trusted with faith unyielding in the days of our
    captivity.
God will lead us forever, renewing us with the glee of youthful
    dancers.
We will possess the portion God set apart for us in ancient
    days.

Leviathan and the wild ox of the mountains will charge and
    contend with each other,
The beast goring fiercely with its horns, the sea monster striking
    with its mighty fins.

But Adonai will make an end of them with His great sword,
And prepare a banquet for the righteous.
They will sit at tables of precious stones, rivers of balsam flowing
    before them.
And they will drink the precious wine stored for them from the
    first of days.

O you upright who have heard the song of God's praise,
may you ever be in the blessed circle of God's faithful.

Through all eternity, exalted be Adonai who conferred true love
    upon us by entrusting to us the Torah.

Jewish Spiritual Kabbalistic/ Hassidic Practices

The goal of all religious practice in Hasidism is *devekut*, – achieving full attachment to God. It is a love of God that is so intense that one who possesses it ultimately cleaves to God. The key Biblical verse relating to *devekut* is *Deuteronomy 11:22* that instructs followers "to love the Lord your God, to walk in all His ways and to **cleave** to Him."

Many practices performed by hasidim and kabbalists are expressions of personal piety that are expressed as part of their spiritual practices and routines (known as *hanhagot* in Hebrew). While some are separate spiritual practices others are enhancements of the *mitzvot*. The following illustrative examples are culled from the volume *Jewish Spiritual Practices* by Yitzhak Buxbaum (Jason Aronson Publishers, date).

UPON ARISING FROM BED

Immediately upon getting out of bed you should arouse yourself to fulfill the mitzvah to fear God, and you should meditate on His greatness, blessed be His name, until you are aroused...You should go to the bathroom then wash your hands and again arouse yourself to fulfill the *mitzvah* to fear God, and think of His greatness and how He is Ruler over all, the center and root of all worlds. Visualize before you the Name and pray to God to illuminate your heart and soul, that the love for Him within you come into revelation, so that you will yearn with love of God and His Torah. (Derech Pikudecha, Preface)

LEAVING THE HOUSE

When you are in your own house you are in a protected environment, where your habits also protect you. But when out on the street, with all its influences and distractions, it is more difficult to be in control of your state of consciousness. This is usually the first big transition of the day. When you leave your house, it is a good practice to kiss the mezuzah and say a brief prayer. The emphasis in such prayers in the tradition is often on being protected from difficulties, both physical and spiritual, which you can meet with in the outside world.

In the morning when you leave your house, put your hand on the mezuzah and say, "Master of the World, have mercy on me and save me from the evil inclination and all its helpers. Amen." (*Derech Hayim, 6–80*)

PREPARATION FOR PRAYER

It is an important thing to see that you learn for at least an hour before each prayer service. Because it is well known that whoever has the ability to sense it, knows that there is a big difference between prayer that comes after Torah learning and that which does not. (*Seder ha-Yom ha-Katzar, p. 5*)

BREATHING MEDITATION

It is possible to use breathing meditation as part of a preparation for prayer. Our breath leads us to think of God, for it is connected with Him and is good evidence of our direct dependence on Him at every moment for our life. The rabbis were led from this thought to the obligation to praise God always. The following is a prayer that can be integrated into a breathing meditation:

O my God, the soul that You have given me is pure You created it, You formed it, You breathed it into me and You keep it within me. And so, as long as my soul is within me, I will thank You and praise You, O Lord my God and the God of my father, Master of all actions, Lord of all souls.

PREPARATION FOR THE MEAL

If a meal is to be made holy and a service to God, you cannot just sit down and eat. You must prepare. Even during the preparation of the food, it is not too early to begin spiritual preparation for the meal by stating your intention by praying:

> "I am cooking this food so that it be for a holy meal and a service of God. My Father in Heaven, let me taste in this food the pleasure of the radiance of the *Shechinah*."

SINGING SONGS

Melody and musical instruments have great power with which to draw a person to God, blessed be He. So, it is good to accustom yourself to enliven yourself frequently with some melody, to bring yourself to joy, and through this to cleave to God, especially on Sabbath and holidays. (*Likkutei Aytzot*, Neginah, #11)

PREPARATION FOR SLEEP

It is a recommended practice that you always carry with you a little notebook in which you can record throughout the day failings and faults, so that at the time set for introspection and *teshuvah* (before bed being a usual time, but there are others) you can go over everything and fix what needs repair.

PREPARATION FOR MAKING LOVE

Arrange for yourself a fixed order of Torah study and prayer each time before you have sexual intercourse. It should be your practice that without this you will never engage in sex. The main thing is that you attach your mind and arouse your feelings during this learning and prayer to a holy *devekut*, immersing yourself fully, according to your ability so that you can come to an awakening of love and fear of God, and of feelings of a holy and pure *teshuvah*. You should also fix for yourself beforehand what to meditate on during the act of intercourse, such as various holy thoughts gathered from different holy books. This will help you to focus yourself and concentrate then on holy thoughts. (*SKV'TZ, p 62b*)

BEING ALONE WITH GOD

Hitbodedut literally means self-seclusion, and is time spent alone with God in prayer, meditation, and self-reflection. Nachman of Bratslav taught that a person should set at least one hour per day for self-seclusion. Following is his advice:

> Strengthen yourself with all your determination to seclude yourself with God each day, for at least an hour, and speak with Him at length about everything that is going on in your life. Confess to Him all your sins, transgressions, and failings, and speak to Him freely as one speaks to a friend. Tell Him about your troubles and everything that is causing you difficulty, and about any bad situation you find yourself in, and that of your family and of the Congregation of Israel. You should speak at length, talk, and talk some more, and argue with Him to convince Him to bring you close to Him, using every argument and every kind of persuasion you can think of.

WHAT TO SAY WHEN ONE MEETS SUFFERING

There are pious phrases that should be in our minds and on our lips as we meet with suffering and difficulties. For example, "Everything that God does is for the good," or "This also is for the good." For losses we suffer: "May God fulfill my lack" – evincing your belief that everything comes from God, and your trust that He will again have mercy on you; or, in the words of Job, "The Lord gave, and the Lord has taken away, blessed be the name of the Lord."

Kabbalah and the Occult

DEMONOLOGY

Jewish mystics utilized motifs found in both the *Talmud* and *Midrash* to develop their system of demonology. They systematized demonology to align it with their understanding of the world. For example, Castilian kabbalists such as Moses de Leon and Jacob Ha-Kohen linked the existence of demons with the last grades of the powers of the "left side" emanation which corresponds in its ten *sefirot* of evil to the ten holy *sefirot*. In contrast, the *Zohar* attributes the origins of certain types of demons in sexual intercourse between humans and demonic powers. The sexual element in the relationship of man and demons holds a prominent place in Zoharic demonology. Demons born out of nightly pollutions are called "the stripes of the children of men" (*Zohar 1:54b*). Feet of the demons are crooked. (*Zohar 3:229b*) Later mystical writings explain that demons born to humans create illegitimate children, called *banim shovavim* (mischievous sons). These sons are prone to come to accompany people at their deaths and to claim their share of their inheritance. *Banim shovavim* also attempt to injure the legitimate children. These notions led to a cemetery custom of circling the dead to repulse the demons.

Lilith is one female demon with a major central position in Jewish demonology. There is even a popular contemporary Jewish feminist magazine named after her. Lilith is often traced to Babylonian demonology, which identifies similar male and female spirits – Lilu and Lilitur.

The first and only biblical reference to Lilith is in the *Book of Isaiah*

34:14, where she is listed as one of the spirits who will lay waste to the land on the day of vengeance:

Wildcats will meet hyenas,
And the satyr shall cry to his fellow
Yea, Lilith shall repose there
And shall find her a place of rest.

Lilith is mentioned several times in the Talmud. For example, in *Eruvin 100b* she appears as a female demon with a woman's face, long hair and wings. We learn in the talmudic tractate *Shabbat 151b* that according to Rabbi Haninah, a person sleeping alone in a house is liable to be seized by Lilith. In the tractate *Baba Batra 73a* we are told that the demon Hormin is one of Lilith's sons.

There are numerous rabbinic legends about Lilith. For instance, in the *Alphabet of Ben Sira*, a tenth-century work, a legend attempts to explain the widespread custom of writing amulets against Lilith. In this work she is identified with the "first Eve," who was created from the earth at the same time as Adam. Unwilling to forgo her equality, she disputed with Adam the manner of their intercourse. Pronouncing God's Name, she flew off into the air. Adam then requested that God send three angels, Sanvei, Sansanavei and Samangalaf after her. Locating her at the Red Sea, the angels threatened that if she did not return one hundred of her sons would die every day. She refused, stating that the very nature of her existence was to harm newborn infants. However, she was forced to swear that whenever she saw the image of those angels in an amulet, she would lose her power over the infant.

In mystical tradition, Lilith has two basic roles: one who strangles children and one who seduces men, producing nocturnal emissions. Through these emissions she bears a never-ending number of demonic children. She is numbered among the four mothers of the demons, the others being Agrat, Machalath, and Naamah. In addition, she becomes the permanent partner of Samael, queen of the realm of the evil forces. In this world of evil, she is the mother of the unholy folk, ruling over all that is impure.

Lilith has also been identified with the Queen of Sheba, based on a Jewish and Arab myth that the Queen of Sheba was a *jinn*, half human, and half demon. Although no one knows for sure the exact reason for this connection, there is a fair amount of conjecture that may well be related to the fact that in the first chapter of the *Book of Job* (1:15) we are told that his seven sons and three daughters were slain by force from Sheba. The *Targum*, the Aramaic translation of the Hebrew Bible, understands Lilith as the instigating force that caused the destruction of Job's children. In Ashkenazic folklore she is depicted as a snatcher of children, a demonic witch, and a seductive dancer.

In the *Kabbalah* (*Zohar, Ra'aya Meheimna III, 227b*) influenced by astrology, Lilith is related to the planet Saturn and all those of a melancholy disposition – of a "black humor" – are her sons.

Beginning in the sixteenth century, people believed that a baby's laughter during sleep was an indication that Lilith was playing with him/her, and that it was therefore advisable to tap on the baby's nose to avert danger.

Eventually, it became common practice to protect women in childbirth from Lilith's great power by placing amulets over the bed or on all four walls of the birthing room. According to *Shimmush Tehillim*, a book dating from the Geonic period, amulets written for women to protect women during childbirth customarily include *Psalm 126* (replaced by *Psalm 121*) and the names of the three angels Sanvei Sansanavei and Samangalaf.

HOW TO AVOID DEMONS

Many actions have been devised through the ages to eradicate and avoid demons. The rabbis regarded wearing *tefillin* (phylacteries), affixing a *mezuzah* to the doorpost of one's house, and donning *tzitzit* (ritual fringes) while directly observing the Law as safeguards against all evil powers (*Talmud Berachot 5a*). *Midrash Rabbah 9:5* states that a priest's blessing protects against evil forces and the *Mishneh of Shabbat 6:2* described wearing amulets for their curative powers. Inscribed amulets, which often contained folded mystical writings, and additional magical symbols were believed to provide protective forces. The creation of amulets and magical incantations as devices to ward off evil spirits has a fascinating literature. Many amulets included various combinations and permutations of the letters of different names of God as well as the names of angels.

Three biblical verses (*Exodus 14:19–21*) were believed to possess strong mystical significance, because each of them consists of seventy-two letters of one of the mysterious names of God. Therefore, these verses were assumed to represent the ineffable Divine Name. They were inserted in the amulets in varied forms as an appeal to God for protection.

The magical word, derived from the Aramaic language, was often used as a formula of incantation against fever or inflammation. Medieval patients were advised to wear an amulet inscribed with this magical word, in the belief that it would ward off and cure diseases. Interestingly, the word *abracadabra* literally means "I will create and I speak." The phrase contains the second word of the Torah, *bara*. The remaining letters all add up to 26, which is the numerical value of YHVH, the four-letter name of God. Thus, in speaking the incantation kabbalists attempted to emulate creation through the speech of God. *Talmud, Pesachim 112a* recommends a similar incantation against the evil forces of blindness (*shabrir*): "My mother has told me to beware of shabriri: shabriri, briri, riri, iri, ri."

THE DYBBUK

There has been a popular belief in Jewish folklore about an evil spirit called a *dybbuk* (meaning a "clinging soul") who can enter a living person and cause them to assume the personality traits of the evil spirit. Belief in the phenomenon of possession became extremely popular during the sixteenth century, especially in the school of Isaac Luria and his chief disciple Chayim Vital.

At first, the *dybbuk* appeared as a demonic spirit that entered the body of a sick person. However, in the past few centuries, the *dybbuk* has become more likely to be understood as the spirit of a sinner who had died and not rested peacefully. Such spirits that take possession of a human body and completely control its personality can only be expelled by the most powerful of exorcisms.

Sephardic kabbalists differentiated between possession by a wandering soul of some deceased Jew (an evil spirit) and possession by a demon. There were different rites of exorcism for each. Unlike evil spirits, demons were distinguished by the following criteria: a demon would coerce a person, make a person twitch hands and feet, and spit up white foam. Evil spirits, on the other hand, would cause a person to feel pain and constrict the heart at will, causing a person to faint.

Not all dybbuks were evil possessors in the strictest sense. Rabbi Chayim Vital recounted the story of a young woman possessed by a spirit, in which a male voice spoke through her claiming to be the spirit of a God-fearing sage who was expelled from the Garden of Eden to perform a short mission in order to atone for a minor transgression. Rabbi Vital interpreted the story as a warning that the Damascan Jews were in extreme danger unless they could be convinced to repent for their sins.

RITUALS FOR JEWISH EXORCISM

By the time that Chayim Vital moved to Damascus from the holy city of Safed in the late fifteenth century, he had associated himself with a small group of mystics who practiced alchemy, chants, and magical incantations, often borrowed from non-Jewish sources. At this time. exorcisms that involved elaborate rituals including smoke and burning sulfur, writing sacred names on parchment, and hanging them around the neck of the host's body, and garbled Latin invocation had become popular. A small number of exorcisms have been preserved in post kabbalistic literature. The following is a sample formula for exorcising an evil spirit composed by Chayim Vital.

> Here is a yichud which my teacher (Luria) taught me, to exorcise an evil spirit (God forbid!); for there are times when the spirit of some evil man, which cannot enter paradise because of its sins,

wanders about the world, and sometimes enters the body of some man or woman, and makes him fall, and this is called epilepsy. (*cholay hanofel*). And by means of this yichud, his (i.e., the sinner's soul) is lifted a bit, and it can leave the man's body. And these are the details, which I myself have tried: I would take the arm of the man and put my hand on his pulse of the right or left hand (for that is the garment of the spirit, and it is clothed therein). And I direct my mind to the spirit clothed in the pulse, that by the power of the yichud I should leave.

While I am still holding the man's arm at the pulse, I say this verse forward and backwards. And I concentrate on the holy names which come from it (e.g., those from the numerical equivalent of each word, and from the initial letters of each word, and from the last letter of each word, as is known.) And during this (i.e., the concentration on the names) I direct my mind that the spirit should exit the body. And then the spirit speaks to you from the body, and tells you anything you might ask, and you should command him to exit.

Sometimes one must blow the shofar near his ear, and meditate on the name *"kera satan"*, (*"tear satan"*) and on it reverse, in *atbash* *"dezeg bant."*

And know that this spirit never comes alone, but a devil supports it, and leads him wandering to complete the recompense for its sins. And he can do nothing without the permission of this devil, for God has appointed him guard over it, as it is written in the Zohar (Bo, 41b): "The evil inclination rules the wicked."

Sometimes the spirit leaves the body, and the devil remains alone to guard the place. Therefore, the roaming spirit does not constantly inhabit the afflicted boy, for it sometimes must leave at appointed times to receive its punishment. Nonetheless, the appointed devil remains to guard the place, and the afflicted person is never healed from his illness, until both exit.

And now I shall copy the text of the Meditation:

Hafkaid alav rash v'satan ya'amid al yemino
Yemino al ya'amid v'satam rasha alav hafkaid.

Onimey la dima'ay natas'vahsar vola diakfah

The order of these vowels follows the order of the vowels of the Sefirot, as it is recorded in Tikkune Zohar [TZ, 70 p. 129). Know, that these seven words, when inverted in the above order, are divine names. I am doubtful if one should meditate on these names when one recites the verse backwards, or perhaps he should read it forwards and backwards, and then meditate on these names: this latter seems more correct.

You should concentrate, that it should leave by the power of all these names. And if he does not exit, repeat the verse, and meditate on all the above names, and after each time say: Leave! Leave! Quickly. Know, that the most important thing is that you should be strong of heart, without any fear; do not have a soft heart, for if you do, he will be strengthened and will not listen to you.

You must also command him not to leave the body from any place except the spot between the nail and flesh of the big toe, so as not to injure the body.

Also, command him by the force of these names which you have meditated, and with excommunication that he may not injure or enter the body of any other Jew.

Know, that when it speaks, the man's body remains mute as a stone, and the spirit's voice comes from the mouth, without any moving of the lips, as a small child-like voice. Also, when the voice comes up from the body to the mouth to speak, the form of some round gland ascends through the neck to the skin of the neck, and again when it descends to the big toe.

Known, furthermore, that when you ask it who it is and what is its name, it will lie and give another name, either to mock you, or so that your command would not take effect (i.e., when you adjure it by name). Therefore, you must adjure him with threats of excommunication, and the power of the Names, not to lie at all, but to tell you who he is with all truth. It is necessary to perform this deed with ritual purity, and ritual immersions, and with holiness and excessive concentration.

To force a demon to leave:

Say the following incantation thirty times in his left ear and thirty times in his right ear, and do not pause between them, and he will leave. Also, if you write it on parchment and hang it around his neck, the demon will leave, or at least it will descend to the foot and will not be able to rise. Seeing that it can no longer ascend, it will leave by itself after a few days. And here is the incantation: *Altinum, Sabtinum, Tanrikum, Sabtinotis, Kintiel, Yah, Hai-Hy, Amen, Amen; Kirlorah, Akhsah, Kalba, Da, V'Reshith, Amen, Amen, Tar.*

(H. Vital, *"Sha'ar Ruach HaKodesh"* (Tel Aviv, 1963), p. 88ff.

THE GOLEM

The golem is a human creature that is created through magic and the use of holy names. The possibility of creating living beings artificially is a widespread belief in the realm of magic. In Judaism, the development of the idea of the golem relates to the magical exegesis of the *Sefer Yetzirah* and the creative power of speech and of the letters.

In the 12th and 13th centuries Hasidei Ashkenaz developed the idea of creating the golem as a mystical ritual used to symbolize the level of their achievement at the conclusion of their studies.

According to the mystics, creating the golem only had symbolic meaning as an ecstatic experience following a festive rite. Participants in this so-called act of creation made a golem out of virgin soil and walked around the figure while reciting the alphabetical letters and the secret Name of God in accordance with a detailed list of instructions. As a result, the golem became animated and lived. When the mystics would walk in the opposite direction and recite the letters in reverse order the golem fell.

According to a Talmudic legend (*Talmud, Shabbat 55a*) the Hebrew word *emet* (truth), which was the seal of the Holy One, was written on the forehead of the golem. When the letter "alef" which began the word *emet* was erased, the remaining word was *met* (dead).

Popular legends about the golem began to emerge, especially in the 15th century. One of the latest and most well-known golem legends relates to Judah Loew ben Bezalel of Prague. According to this legend, Rabbi Loew created the golem so that it would serve him but was forced to restore him to dust when the golem began to go wild and endanger peoples' lives.

ASTROLOGY

Astrology is the study of the influence of the positions and relationships of the sun, moon, stars, and planets on human actions. The belief that the planets and stars influenced the fate of human beings stemmed from ancient Babylonia. The Israelite Prophets, who were aware of the customs and practices of the star gazers (in Hebrew, *chovray ha-shamayim*) among the Babylonians and other Near Eastern peoples, attacked their predictions as futile.

Nevertheless, many Talmudic rabbis believed that the heavenly bodies played a role in determining human affairs in the sublunar world. For instance, Abraham and his progeny are spoken of as having been elevated beyond subjection to the stars (*Genesis Rabbah 44:12*), yet the blessing bestowed upon the patriarch in *Genesis 24:1* is interpreted in the *Tosefta* of *Kiddushin* 5:17 as the gift of astrology.

The words used by the ancient rabbis contain traces of the ancient belief that stars can hold influence over people. The most familiar example of this is the expression *mazal tov*, which is usually translated as "good luck." However, the phrase literally refers to "a good star." In several talmudic passages it is stated that every person has a celestial body or a particular star (*i.e.*, a *mazal*), that is his or her patron from conception through birth, and which perceives things unknown even to the person himself. For example, the Talmudic tractate of *Shabbat 53b* discusses planetary influence on human beings, and the Talmudic tractate of *Megillah 3a* states that if a person is seized with fright (although he sees nothing) that his star sees, and the recitation of the *Shema* prayer is a remedy. The Talmudic tractate of *Nedarim 39b* describes the phenomenon of two people born under the same star as sharing both a bodily and spiritual kinship, whereas the midrash of *Genesis Rabbah 1:6* fully describes the connection of certain constellation of stars, including those of Pleiades and Orion, as influencing the growth and the ripening of fruits.

Medieval Jewish scholars who were versed in astrology and considered it a true science include Saadia Gaon, whose commentary on *Sefer Yetzirah* contains astrological material, Solomon ibn Gabirol, whose *Keter Malchut* included an account of the influence of each of the seven planets, and Abraham ibn Daud, whose book *Emunah Ramah* argues that the positions of the stars were set at the time of creation and that predictions can be made on the basis of them.

The mystical work *Sefer Yetzirah* contains several astrological passages of interest. One describes the relationship of the seven Hebrew consonants that take a *dagesh* to the seven planets and the seven days of the week, and the relationship of the twelve simple consonants to the twelve houses of the zodiac and the twelve months. *Sefer Raziel* contains the main basis for the systematic study of astrology. For example:

> "How can the seers know what a person's life will be as soon as one is born? The ruling planet ascended in the East (at the hour of birth) in his wife's house. If the house of Saturn is in ascension, that person will live to be 57, if it is the house of Jupiter, one will live 79 years. Saturn presides over well-being, happiness, riches, honor, greatness, and royalty. Mars presides over blood and the sword, Venus over attractiveness, grace and appetite."

The *Zohar* takes astrology quite for granted. For example, it is stated (*Ki Tetze* 3, 281b, *Raya Meheimna*) that "all the stars and the constellations in the heavens were appointed to be rulers and commandments over the world. There is not even one single blade of grass in the entire world over which a star or a planet does not preside." *Pinchas 216b* states that all earthly creatures were dependent on the stars prior to the giving of the Torah. However, after revelation at Sinai, God exempted those Israelite children who studied and observed God's Law from the rule of the stars, whereas the skeptics and ignorant ones were not absolved.

CHIROMANCY

Chiromancy is the art of determining a person's character and fate from lines and marks on their palms and fingers. The first Jewish mention of chiromancy first appears in the circle of Merkavah mysticism. Fragments of this literature include a chapter called *Hakkarat Panim le-Rabbi Yishmael* which is one of the earliest literary references to chiromancy.

According to Gershom Scholem, the German-born Israeli philosopher and historian who was widely regarded as the founder of the modern, academic study of Kabbalah, the Merkavah mystics used chiromancy to ascertain a person's fitness to receive esoteric teaching. They quoted *Genesis 5:1–2* as scriptural support for this "science": "This is the book of the generations of man" (the Hebrew *toldot* [generations] interpreted to mean "the book of man's character and fate") and "male and female created He them", which implies that chiromantic prediction varies according to sex, the right hand being the determining factor for the male, and the left hand for the female.

At the end of the 13th century, the kabbalist Menachem Recanati referenced a volume entitled *Sefer ha-Atidot* (Book of the Future), which is based on the principles of the astrological method of chiromancy relating the main line of the palm and the various parts of the hand to the seven planets and their influences.

Further evidence of the chiromantic tradition among the early mystics is found in *Sefer Haminhagot* (Book of Customs), the work of the 12th century sage Asher ben Samuel who relates that the mystics used to examine the lines of the palms of the hands in order to determine a man's fate at the conclusion of the Sabbath.

Various parts of the *Zohar* itself includes passages focusing on the lines of the hand and the forehead such as in *Tikkunei Zohar* which establishes a relationship between the lines on a man's hand and forehead and the transmigrations of his soul. Hebrew books on astrological chiromancy named the main lines of the hand as follows: 1. *Kav Hachayim* (lifeline) 2. *Kav Hachochmah* (line of wisdom) 3. *Kav Hashulchan* (table line) 4. *Kav Hamazal* (line of fate) 5. *Kav Habri'ut* (line of health).

The belief that that their master Isaac Luria was an expert in chiromancy spread among his students.

THE ANGEL METATRON

One angel, Metatron, is accorded a distinctive role in Jewish angelology and it plays a significant role in the Talmud and in Jewish mysticism. The origin of Metatron's name is obscure, but suggestions regarding its origin include from the word *matar* meaning "keeper of the watch"; from the word *metator* meaning "messenger"; from the combination of the Greek words *meta* and *thronos* meaning "one who serves behind the throne."

Metatron is mentioned in several places in the *Talmud*. In the tractate of *Hagigah 15a*, Elisha ben Avuyah saw Metatron seated and said that "perhaps there are two powers," as though indicating that Metatron himself is a second deity. The *Talmud* goes on to explain that Metatron was given permission to be seated because of his position as celestial scribe recording the good deeds of Israel.

In another *Talmudic* story (*Sanhedrin 38b*) Metatron is described as the angel of God referred to in *Exodus 23:21* of whom it was said, "do not listen to his voice."

Yet another tradition associates Metatron with Enoch who "walked with God" (*Genesis 5:22*) and who ascended to heaven, thus transforming from a human being to a celestial being. His roles were diverse, and included ministering to the Throne of Glory, acting as Temple high priest, acting as a minister of wisdom, and keeping charge of the guardian angels.

Kabbalists have often been known to identity Metatron with the Supreme emanation of light from the *Shechinah*. Other kabbalists identify Metatron with the angel of Enoch who ascended to heaven. The *Zohar* describes this transformation, stating that the Divine spark which God placed into Adam, the first human being, left his body after having sinned by eating of the Tree of Knowledge. The spark entered the body of Enoch, perfecting him to the point that he needed to be transported to heaven, and there he metamorphised into the angel of Metatron.

Although later literature relating to Metatron is scattered, students of angelology widely agree that there is hardly a duty in the celestial realm and within the dominion of one angel among the other angels in which Metatron is not involved.

Life after Life in
Kabbalistic Thought

The need to explain the mystery of life and the difference between life and death may have prompted human beings' first thoughts regarding the soul. Ancient philosophies postulated that anima or spirits gave life to matter. The departure of these spirits left matter inert or dead. Whether we term it animal, spirit, soul, or breath of life, the basic idea is the same: a life-giving force enters and departs from matter. This force transcends, survives, and exists independently of matter.

The *Zohar* assumes that the human soul has a three-fold nature. Medieval philosophers such as Maimonides and Abraham ibn Ezra envisioned the soul as having three dimensions, which they labeled *nefesh* (vegetative soul), *ruach* (animal soul) and *neshamah* (intellectual soul). This was the dominant model of the soul espoused by the kabbalists,

Nefesh, lowest level animated and preserved the soul. It comes into being at birth and is the first element found in any individual.

Ruach the soul's second level, is portrayed in the *Zohar* as an intermediary power which animates the *nefesh*, utilizing the light that emanates from the *neshamah*.

Neshamah, a supernal level of the soul, is aroused by studying Torah and performing *mitzvot*, allowing one to perceive divine mysteries.

The author of *Raaya Meheimna* describes two additional dimensions of the soul – *chayah* and *yechidah, which* represent the most sublime levels of intuitive cognition. Only a few specially chosen individuals are endowed with these capabilities.

According to the *Zohar*, the *nefesh* remains in the grave with the body after a person's death, often undergoing judgment and suffering punishment. Subsequently the *ruach* goes through its own phase of judgment in the netherworld, where it too is punished for its sins over the period of a year. In phase three, the *ruach* enters a realm called Lower Gan Eden. *Neshamah* is not liable to transgression and returns to its source in the Upper Gan Eden where it experiences forms of divine bliss. Finally, the higher faculties of the soul, *chayah* and *yechidah* remain in contact with the Godhead after death.

Although Kabbalistic systems vary greatly with regard to the details of reward and punishment, the variations do not affect the principle of immortality of the soul or its designation for eternal life. Visions about what happens to the different parts of the soul after their separation from the body vary because each one undergoes individual refinements and purifications and ascends to a different place in the supernal world. However, there is a common belief that all the parts of the soul will return and become unified with the resurrection of the dead and will remain connected to the total spiritual unity from that time forward.

REINCARNATION

Reincarnation is the belief that a soul enters another living entity after the death of its body. A popular idea in Hinduism and in ancient Greek philosophy, the belief is generally limited to mystics and Hasidim within Judaism. Kabbalists viewed the purpose of reincarnation as an opportunity for the soul to cleanse itself of impurities.

The Hebrew term for reincarnation is *gilgul neshamot*, literally the "turning" of souls." The idea of transmigration of the soul appears to have been widely accepted in kabbalistic circles by the 12th century. Believers in reincarnation posit that souls have an independent life, existing before and after the death of the body. The soul joins with the body at an appropriate time, and remains with it for a specific period, then takes leave of the body at the time of death.

There is widespread recognition that not all righteous individuals in this world receive their due rewards. Some suffer, even though they are righteous. For kabbalists, reincarnation seemed a possible answer to this "injustice." They argued that the suffering of a righteous person in this world is not a result of personal sins but rather a consequence of acts committed in a previous incarnation. This idea helped explain the tragic death of young children. Their early death, posited kabbalists, was the result of transgressions committed by an ancestor in an earlier *gilgul*. It was therefore not the child that was being punished, but rather the soul of the previous sinner.

While some kabbalists believed reincarnation applied exclusively to human beings, others held that animals and even inanimate objects could also be reincarnated.

GILGUL, IBBUR AND DYBBUK

The kabbalists identified three types of reincarnation: *gilgul, ibbur and dybbuk. Gilgul* takes place during pregnancy. *Ibbur* (impregnation), a benign type of possession, occurs when an old soul enters the body of another person at any time during that person's lifetime, and performs certain commandments for a period of time. A *dybbuk* ("clinging soul") is an evil soul who invades another person, causing the person to change his or her personality. Originally a *dybbuk* was thought to be a demon that possessed the fragile body of a sick person. Later, some *dybbuks* were also thought to be the spirits of dead people who were not laid to rest. As the doctrine of *gilgul* spread, the *dybbuk* came to be seen as a wicked soul, unable to transmigrate, who would possess selective, weakened individuals, often for vengeance.

As folktales about various *dybbuks* began to proliferate, some found their way into literary expression. S. Ansky, author and folklorist of the early twentieth century, was the author of the most famous dybbuk story, his Yiddish play *Der Dybbuk*. It was later translated into Hebrew by Chayim Nachman Bialik and performed by the Israeli theater troupe *Habimah* in Moscow, Tel Aviv, and New York. In 1938 a Polish-Yiddish company produced a film version of the play. In the story Chanan, a Yeshivah student, falls in love with Leah, daughter of the wealthy merchant Reb Sender. Chanan wants to marry her, but the girl's father arranges for her to marry a wealthier person. Chanan, in a desperate attempt to become wealthy, turns to kabbalistic magic, which drives him to madness and ultimately to his death. Leah begins to frequent the cemetery where Chanan is buried, and on the eve of her wedding becomes possessed by Chanan's soul. Her father consults with a rebbe, who then dreams of a meeting with the spirit of Chanan's father. The father tells him that Sender and he were once close friends who had pledged their yet unborn children in marriage if they should happen to be a boy and a girl. Chanan's father dies, and Sender forgets his vow. Chanan's father now demands justice from a rabbinical court, which rules that lives of unborn cannot be pledged, and that Sender must now do penance. An exorcism is performed, and the *dybbuk* (Chanan's spirit) eventually withdraws from Leah's body. Leah's soul also departs to join her dead lover in eternal wandering.

Mystics still defend the idea of reincarnation in modern times. For example, Philip S. Berg, an Orthodox rabbi who is dean of the Research Center of Kabbalah International, has argued that reincarnation is not a question of faith or doctrine but of logic and reason.

RESURRECTION

Kabbalists also embraced the doctrine of resurrection of the dead. They believe that at the end of days, following the Great Day of Judgment, the perfected soul will re-enter a fully resurrected body. The doctrine of Israel's messianic redemption relates to the doctrine of resurrection. They derive support from the biblical verses: "I will open your graves and bring you out of your graves" (*Ezekiel 37:12*) and "Your dead shall live, their corpses shall rise; awake and sing, you who lie in the dust" (*Isaiah 26:19*). interpreting these verses in the sense of a national restoration. In their view Ezekiel predicts the dead nation (of Israel) will come to life again. In his striking vision in Chapter 37, Ezekiel is transported into a valley of dry bones. As he prophesies to them, they come together into complete skeletons, which become covered with flesh and skin. Then the wind blows upon the inanimate bodies and they come to life. Kabbalists interpret this prophecy to the revival of the dead nation to which the scattered remains (of the exiles) return.

The belief in the resurrection of the body, in contradistinction to the immortality of the soul, became a fundamental doctrine of the Pharisees during the Second Commonwealth. They believed that the soul and the body would be reunited in the future world, reconstituting the original person who would stand in judgment before God and receive reward or punishment according to his good or bad conduct during life.

Maimonides the medieval philosopher incorporated the belief in resurrection in his Thirteen Principles of Faith and wrote a special treatise on the subject to disprove those who accused him of heresy regarding this doctrine.

Current belief in resurrection, held today by many Orthodox and some Conservative Jews, was central to rabbinic Judaism. Today it has once again surfaced among some liberal Jews, who affirm it with a sense of authenticity.

Gematria

Gematria is the mystical method of disclosing the hidden meaning of a biblical or other text by reckoning the numerical equivalents of its Hebrew letters. The Babylonians and the Greeks also used letters to signify numbers. Numerical *gematria* first appears in the rabbinic literature of 2nd century sages.

Unlike Arabic or Roman languages, Hebrew has no numerals. Instead, each letter of the Hebrew alphabet corresponds to a numerical value. For example, *alef* is one, *bet* is two, *gimel* is three, and so forth. The corresponding letter is added to each decimal unit to express numbers larger than 10. For example, 12 is *yud-bet* (*yud* = 10 plus bet = 2) and 25 is *kaf-hay* (kaf = 20 plus hay = 5). The only exceptions are 15 and 16 which are written *tet-vav* (9 plus 6) and *tet-zayin* (9 plus 7) respectively, to avoid the combination of the *yud* with the *hay* or *vav* which forms God's Name and is therefore prohibited.

Examples of the some of the more popular forms of *gematria* systems follow.

FORM I

In this gematrical from the numerical value of one word (equaling the sum of the numerical value of all its letters) is equal to that of another word. For example:

According to *Genesis 14:14* Abraham had 318 trained servants. This number equals the sum of the letters spelling the name *Eliezer*, the servant of Abraham mentioned in *Genesis 15:2*. (Talmud *Nedarim* 32a)

The ladder reaching from heaven to earth that appeared in Jacob's dream referred to *Sinai*, since the numerical value of *sulam* (ladder) equals 130, equal to the numeric value of *Sinai*. This is interpreted to mean that the Torah, which was revealed at Mount Sinai, is the ladder that leads from earth to heaven.

The numerical value of the Hebrew word *echad* (one) is 13, which is equivalent to the Hebrew word for love (*ahavah*), which is interpreted as an indication that the highest purpose that a person should try to attain is the love of God, who is One.

FORM II

According to this form, the *gematria* of a word is calculated from the numerical value of the letters squared.

For example, the tetragrammaton *YHVH* (the four-letter Name of God) consists of the number equivalents 10, 5, 6 and 5, the sum of whose squares is 186 (*i.e.*, 100 + 25 + 36 + 25). This is numerically equivalent to the Hebrew word *makom* which means "place." Thus, the word *Makom* refers to God as the Omnipresent God. (*i.e.*, God is in every place).

FORM III

A third form of *gematriah* interprets a word or phrase in terms of the significance of its numerical equivalent. For example:

In the book of *Genesis 12:1* the numerical equivalent of the Hebrew words *lech lecha* meaning "go forth" is 100, which alludes to the fact that Abraham was 100 years old when his wife Sarah gave birth to their son Isaac.

Genesis 18:18 states that Abraham shall become (in Hebrew, *yihiyeh*) a great nation. The number value of *yihiyeh* (30) mystically alludes to the belief that in every generation there are 30 saints who are as righteous as Abraham.

FORM IV

The fourth form of *gematria* interprets words by using the numerical equivalent of each letter to signify something specific. For example:

> The Hebrew name *Yitzchak* (Isaac) is composed of the Hebrew letters *yud, tzaddi, chet* and *kuf*. The *yud*, valued at 10, refers to the 10 trials by which Abraham was tested according to rabbinic legend. The *tzaddi*, valued at 90 refers to Sarah's age when she gave birth to Isaac. The *Chet*, valued at 8 refers to the eighth day on which Abraham's son Isaac was circumcised. The *kuf*, valued at 100 refers to Abraham's age when his son Isaac was born.
>
> The Hebrew word *tzedakah* means, righteousness and has been interpreted in reference to prayer. Its first letter *tzaddi* (numerical value 90) refers to the 90 amens. (the number of daily "amens" that a righteous person, called a *tzaddik*, says). Its second letter *dalet* (numerical value 4) refers to the four prayers that sanctify God in the daily liturgy. The third letter *kuf* (numerical value 100) equals the exact number of blessings per day required according to rabbinic law. The final letter (numerical value 5) refers to the Five Books of Moses (Tikkunei Zohar 19:40b).

OTHER APPLICATIONS

Mystics use *gematria* to find hidden meaning in verses and texts in many additional ways. For example:

> Each of the parents escorting brides and grooms at traditional Jewish weddings customarily carry a lit candle in the procession as a sign of joy and honor. The two candles accompanying the bridal pair are considered particularly auspicious because the numerical value of *ner* (Hebrew for candle, numerical value 250) multiplied

by 2 (*i.e.*, 500) is equal to the numerical value of the biblical phrase *pru ur'vu* (be fruitful and multiply). Thus, the candles represent the parents' wish for their children to successfully build a family.

When he awakens from his dream of the angels descending and ascending the ladder Jacob says: "*Yesh Adonai bamakom hazeh*" (God is in this place)" (*Genesis 28:10 ff*). The numerical value of these Hebrew words is 541, equal to the numerical value of the Hebrew name of Israel (*Yisrael*) which is taken as God's promise of the Land of Israel to the Jewish people.

Isaac Luria taught that one should dip the bread in salt three times before eating it because the word for God (*YHVH* pronounced *Adonai*) has the numerical value of 26. Three times 26 is equivalent to 78, the *gematria* for both *melach* (salt) and *lechem* (bread).

It is customary to read the book of *Ruth* on the festival of *Shavuot* because the numerical value of the Hebrew letters in Ruth's name total 606, the number of precepts that Ruth accepted as a proselyte on her conversion to Judaism. Added to the 7 Noachian precepts (which previously were Ruth's only responsibility), the total equals 613, the exact number of *mitzvot* (religious obligations) in the Torah.

The last letter of the Hebrew word *shema* is an *ayin*, which has the numerical value of 70. According to the Zohar, the letter *ayin* represents the seventy different forces of creation which are manifest in the seventy nations of the world and the seventy languages, as well as the seventy descendants who accompanied Jacob to Egypt. In listening to the message of unity in the *Shema*, one brings these seventy forces into the ear and mind and unifies them with God.

God's revelation to Moses in the burning bush (*Exodus 3*) was believed to provide Moses with a mystical foreshadowing of his age at death. The Hebrew word for bush is *sneh*, which has the numerical value of 120. Moses died at age 120!

Kabbalistic Meditation

The term "meditation" (*hitbonenut*) first appears in kabbalistic literature from the middle of the 13th century, referring to protracted concentration of thought on supernal lights of the divine world and of the spiritual worlds in general. A highly detailed elaboration of the doctrine and concept of meditation can be found in the teachings of the great mystic Abraham Abulafia. His entire volume *Chochmat HaTzeruf* (science of combination) was devoted to teaching a safe approach to meditation. Many works by other early kabbalists contain instruction about methods of meditation, and these methods endured after the expulsion from Spain among kabbalists who were influenced by Abulafia. The most detailed textbook on meditation regarding the mystery of the *sefirot* is *Even ha-Shoham* by Joseph ibn Sayah of Damascus, written in Jerusalem in 1538. The kabbalists of Safed continued to set considerable store in meditation, as is evident from Eleazar Azikri's *Sefer Charedim* (Venice, 1601) and Moses Cordovero's *Pardes Rimmonim* (Cracow, 1592).

Modern-day Jewish meditative practices include the following:

EXTERNALLY DIRECTED MEDITATIONS

Mantra

Mantras, words repeated for a designated period, are the best-known types of external-directed meditations. They were practiced by early kabbalistic schools. For example, *Heichalot*, (visions of acent) begins with the repetition of several Divine Names 112 times.

Contemplation

In this practice one gazes and concentrates on a particular object or visual image. The *tetragrammaton* (four-letter name for God *YHVH*). Is the simplest contemplative device in kabbalah This practice reached its zenith under the influence of Rabbi Shalom Sharabi, an 18th century mystic.

Yichudim

Yichudim (Unifications) was a central practice for followers of the Ari (explain who he was). This practice involved contemplating a mental image, usually consisting of combinations of Divine names.

INTERNALLY DIRECTED MEDITATION

Internally Directed Meditation focuses on thoughts, feelings, or mental images that arise spontaneously in the mind. Rav Nachman of Bratslav applied this methodology by verbalizing thoughts while keeping them concentrated on a single focus through spontaneous prayer.

NON-DIRECTED MEDITATION

This type of meditation strives for stillness of the mind and withdrawal from internal and external perception. It was practiced by Dov Baer of Mezerich and Levi Yitzchak of Berdichev.

MEANS OF MEDITATION

Kabbalists employ various means of meditation including:

Intellect

Common among the so-called theoretical kabbalists, this method involved contemplating various aspects of Torah, often probing the many meanings of the commandments. Contemporary Hasidim often use this method to achieve an elevated state of religious ecstasy.

Study of devotional works

Kabbalist study devotional works, contemplating each concept with intense concentration with the goal of self-improvement. This method was popular among followers of the Musar movement of the 19th century.

Path of emotions

Particularly important in the Hassidic schools, kavanah-meditation uses formal daily prayers as a kind of mantra. The practitioner is taught to imbue the words of their prayers with all of their feelings and emotions in order to divest themselves from the physical (known as *hitpashtut ha-gashmiut*). This path is also found in meditation involving the use of music.

Path combining intellect and emotions in the path of love

According to Maimonides, when people deeply contemplate God, they become aware of God's wisdom and are brought to a passionate love of God. He further asserts that such a love for God can be so intense that it literally draws one's soul out of the body. This occurs when a saint dies by "the kiss of God."

Path of the body

This form of meditation that employs body motions and breathing exercises played a key role in the meditation system of the mystic Abraham Abulafia. Today it finds expression in the Hassidic practice of swaying and fervent bowing fervently as well as dancing during prayer.

Notable Advice and Quotations

The following is a compilation of topical advice from the books of the *Zohar* as well as the writings of Rav Nachman of Bratslav.

AGED
The prosperity of a country is in accordance with its treatment of the elderly. (*Nachman of Bratslav*)

ANGER
An angry person is unfit to pray. (*Nachman of Bratslav*)

COMMUNICATION WITH GOD
The person who wishes to sing to God in a loud voice should possess one pleasant to others. Otherwise, such a person ought to refrain from praying aloud. (*Zohar I, 249b*)

COMPASSION
When there is no compassion, crime increases. (*Nachman of Bratslav*)

CONFESSION:
If a person confesses his sins, he cannot be brought to judgment. (*Zohar IV, 231a*)

EATING
Regard your dining table as the table before God. Chew well, and do not hurry. (*Zohar IV, 246a*)

ENVY
A person who is envious is guilty of robbery in thought. (*Nachman of Bratslav*)

EVIL IMPULSE
When a person has learned to subdue his chief enemy, the evil impulse, that person finds it easier to conquer all other enemies. (*Taikune Zohar 178a*)

FAITH
There can be no faith without truth. (*Zohar III*)

FEARING GOD
The greatest reward in the future world is reserved for the person who teaches his children how to fear God and to serve God in the ways of the Torah. (*Zohar I, 188a*)

FLATTERY
Flattery leads to vulgarity. The flatterer is ultimately despised. (*Nachman of Bratslav*)

FOOLISHNESS
What is the sign of a foolish person? One who talks too much. (*Zohar IV, 193b*)

GOD AND WORDS OF TORAH
If words of Torah are spoken at a meal, it is as if God has shared in it. (*Zohar II, 154a*)

HONOR
Be more careful of your neighbor's honor than of your own person. (*Zohar Hadash to Song of Songs, 61a*)

HUMILITY
God is a friend of the person who is humble. (*Zohar II, 233b*)

LEADERSHIP
The acts of the leader are the acts of the nation. If the leader is just,

the nation is just. If the leader is unjust, the nation too is unjust and is punished for the sins of the leader. (*Zohar II, 47a*)

LIGHT

Israel is like a wick, the Torah is its oil, and the *Shechinah* is its light. (*Tikkune Zohar, 21*)

LUCK

According to luck, no person should live over seventy years. However, God adds to one's years if God desires to do so. (*Zohar I, 257b*)

MARRIAGE

When there is no union of male and female, men are not worthy of beholding the Divine Presence. (*Zohar III, 59a*)

MIRACLES

Believe in God through faith, and not because of miracles. (*Nachman of Bratslav*)

OATHS

What is a desirable oath? If the evil impulse is leading you away from the performance of a commandment, take an oath that you will perform it. (*Zohar II, 91b*)

KNOWLEDGE

Knowledge that is paid for will no longer be remembered. (*Nachman of Bratslav*)

MITZVOT

A person is respected on high according to the way he performs all the positive commandments in fear and in love. (*Tikkune Zohar, 70, 175b*)

PARENTS

Honor your father and your mother just as you honor God, for all three have been partners in your creation. (*Zohar III, 93a*)

PIETY

Who are the pious? They who consider each day as their last on earth and repent accordingly. (*Zohar I, 220a*)

PROPHETS

Compared to Moses, all the prophets were like the moon compared to the sun. (*Zohar IV, 135b*)

QUARRELS

The world stands firm because of those who close their lips during a quarrel. (*Nachman of Bratslav*)

POVERTY

Woe to the person against whom the poor person makes complaint to his Heavenly Master, for the poor person is nearest to the King. (*Zohar II, 86b*)

REBUKE

The person who rebukes his friend with love, always do so privately, so that the offender is not publicly embarrassed. (*Zohar III, 46a*)

SIN

If a person sins in secret, God takes pity on him. If he repents, God forgives him and forgets his transgression. If there is no repentance, God makes his sin public. (*Zohar I, 66a*)

SYNAGOGUE

The person who comes to the synagogue early and leaves late merits a goodly portion. (*Zohar I, 256a*)

Woe to the person who converses in the synagogue. Such a person demonstrates that he does not belong there. (*Zohar I, 256a*)

WINE

If you wish to keep your business a secret, do not drink wine. (*Zohar IV, 177b*)

WISDOM

There is no Torah without wisdom, and there is no wisdom without Torah. (*Zohar III, 81a*)

Glossary

Aliyat Neshamah: Ascent of the soul (*i.e.*, mystical exaltation)

Atzilut: Emanation. Overflow of divine essence from the *Ein Sof*.

Binah: Understanding. The third *sefirah*.

Baal-Shem: A mystic who possessed secret knowledge of God's Name and could use it for purposes of healing.

Chochmah: Wisdom. Second sefirah.

Chochmat Hatzeruf: Science of the combination of letters.

Chochmat Neestera: Mystical secret wisdom.

Devekut: Mystical clinging to God and union with the sefirot.

Din: Judgment. The fifth *sefirah*.

Ein Sof: God's mystical infiniteness.

Gashmiyut: Corporeality.

Gematriah: System of numerology in which number values are assigned to letters of the Hebrew alphabet to uncover hidden meanings of words and texts.

Gilgul: Transmigration of souls; reincarnation.

Golem: Artificially made human.

Hanhagot: Spiritual practices.

Heichalot: A genre of literature that provides the literary source for the mystical focus on emotional and ecstatic experiences.

Hesed: (Mercy). Fourth *sefirah*.

Hitbodedut: Self seclusion.

Hitlahavut: Religious enthusiasm.

Hod: Majesty. Eighth *sefirah*.

Ibbur: State in which a guardian soul of one individual attaches to another individual.

Kavanah: Mystical concentration.

Kabbalah: Jewish mystical movement.

Keter: Crown. First *sefirah*.

Kelippot: According to *kabbalah*, shells or husks which are forces of evil that dominate the spiritual lights originally emanating from creation.

Ma'aseh Bereshit: Literally "the act of the creation of the world." Refers to a specific school of mystical thought that speculates about the creation of the world.

Ma'aseh Merkavah: Literally, "the word of the chariot." Also called *merkavah* mysticism. Refers to apocalyptic visions and a mystical perception of the throne of God in its chariot, as described in the first chapter of the book of *Ezekiel*.

Malchut: Kingship. Also known as the *Shechinah*. Tenth *sefirah*.

Nefesh: Lowest level of the soul.

Neshamah: Highest level of the soul.

Netzach: Triumph. Seventh *sefirah*.

Niggun: Melody without words.

Resurrection: Notion that at the end of days the body will arise and be joined with the soul.

Ruach: Middle level of the soul.

Sefirot: Ten mystical aspects of God.

Shechinah: Feminine aspect of God. Tenth *sefirah*.

Shevirat Hakelim: Breaking of the vessels.

Tiferet: Splendor. Sixth *sefirah*.

Tikkun: Mystical repair of the shattered world.

Tzaddik: A righteous individual, also used to refer to leaders of the Hasidic dynasties.

Tzimtzum: Contraction of God.

Yesod: Foundation. Ninth *sefirah*.

Yichud: Unity: Unification among the *sefirot*.

Yoday Chen: Those familiar with kabbalistic literature, its symbols and philosophy.

Zivug: Union. Union of human soul and the *Shechinah*.

For Further Reading

Abelson, J. *Jewish Mysticism*. New York: Sepher-Hermon Press, 1981.

Ariel, David S. *The Mystic Quest: An Introduction to Jewish Mysticism*. New Jersey: Jason Aronson, 1988.

Bokser, Ben Zion, ed. *The Jewish Mystical Tradition*. New Jersey: Jason Aronson 1993.

Buxbaum Yitzhak. *Jewish Spiritual Practices*. New Jersey: Jason Aronson, 1990.

Gillman, Neil. *The Death of Death*. Vermont: Jewish Lights, 1997.

Idel, Moshe. *Kabbalah: New Perspectives*. Connecticut: Yale University Press, 1988.

Kaplan, Aryeh. *Meditation and Kabbalah*. New Jersey: Jason Aronson, 1995.

Matt, Daniel C. *The Heart of Jewish Mysticism*. New York: Harper Collins. 1995.

Pinson, DovBer. *Reincarnation and Judaism: The Journey of the Soul*. New Jersey: Jason Aronson, 1999.

Raphael, Simcha Paull. *Jewish Views of the Afterlife*. New Jersey: Jason Aronson, 1994.

Scholem, Gershom. *Kabbalah*. Jerusalem: Keter Publishing, 1974.